Guide to
MANAGERIAL COMMUNICATION

Guide to

Managerial Communication

Effective Business Writing and Speaking

Fourth Edition

by Mary Munter
Amos Tuck School of Business
Dartmouth College

PRENTICE HALL
Upper Saddle River, NJ 07458

Library of Congress Cataloging-in-Publication Data

Munter, Mary.
Guide to managerial communication: effective business writing and speaking/Mary Munter.— 4th ed.
p. cm.
Includes bibliographical references and index.
ISBN 0-13-256447-5
1. Business communication. 2. Communication in management. I. Title.
HF5718.M86 1997
658.4'5—dc21 97-9000
CIP

Acquisitions Editor: Don Hull
Assistant Editor: John Larkin
Editorial Assistant: Jim Campbell
Editor-in-Chief: James Boyd
Director of Development: Steve Deitmer
Marketing Manager: John Chillingworth
Production Editor: Kelly Warsak
Production Coordinator: Renee Pelletier
Managing Editor: Valerie Q. Lentz
Manufacturing Buyer: Kenneth J. Clinton
Manufacturing Supervisor: Arnold Vila
Manufacturing Manager: Vincent Scelta
Design Director: Patricia Wosczyk
Interior Design: Ann France
Cover Director: Jayne Conte
Cover Design: Kiwi Design
Composition: Accu-color Inc./Beaumont

A Simon & Schuster Company
Upper Saddle River, New Jersey 07458

ISBN 0-13-256447-5

Prentice-Hall International (UK) Limited, *London*
Prentice-Hall of Australia Pty. Limited, *Sydney*
Prentice-Hall Canada, Inc., *Toronto*
Prentice-Hall Hispanoamericana, S.A., *Mexico*
Prentice-Hall of India Private Limited, *New Delhi*
Prentice-Hall of Japan, Inc., *Tokyo*
Simon & Schuster Asia Pte. Ltd., *Singapore*
Editora Prentice-Hall do Brasil, Ltda., *Rio de Janeiro*

Printed in the United States of America

10 9 8 7 6 5

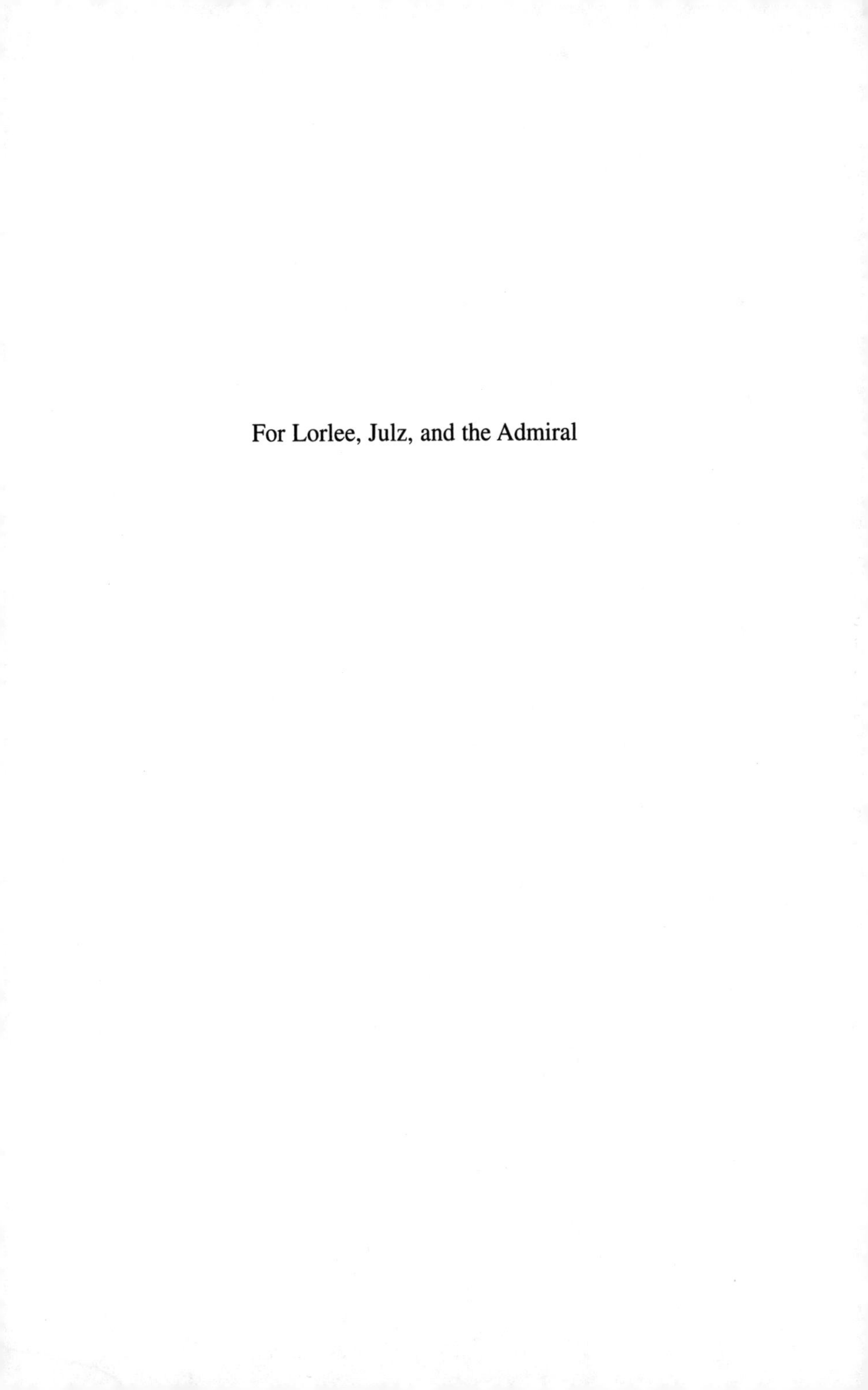

For Lorlee, Julz, and the Admiral

Contents

Introduction

HOW THIS BOOK CAN HELP YOU

If you are facing a specific managerial communication problem, turn to the relevant part of this book for guidance. For example:

- You're speaking or writing to a new group of people. How can you enhance your credibility? How can you appeal to them?
- You can't get started on a writing project. How can you overcome writer's block?
- The thought of giving that presentation next week is making you nervous. What can you do to relax?
- In making your case, you don't know whether to start with your recommendation or to build up to it. Which is more persuasive?
- Your new computer programs can create terrific visual aids and writing formats. How can you get the most out of them?
- Your boss is returning your memos and reports to you to rewrite. How can you organize your ideas? How can you express yourself more succinctly?
- You're wasting time at meetings. How can you get more accomplished?

If you don't have a specific question, but need general guidelines, procedures, and techniques, read through this entire book. For example:

- You would like a framework for thinking strategically about all managerial communication.
- You would like to know more about the process of writing and editing more efficiently.

- You would like a step-by-step procedure for preparing an oral presentation.

If you are taking a professional training course, a college course, a workshop, or a seminar, use this book as a reference.

- You may very well be a good communicator already. You would like, however, to polish and refine your managerial writing and speaking skills by taking a course or seminar.

WHO CAN USE THIS BOOK

This book is written for you if you need to speak or write in a managerial, business, government, or professional context—that is, if you need to achieve results with and through other people. You probably already know these facts:

- *You spend most of your time at work communicating.* Various studies show that 50 to 90 percent of work time is spent in some communication task.
- *Your success is based on communication.* Other studies verify that your career advancement is correlated with your ability to communicate well.
- *Communication is increasingly important today.* Recent trends, such as increased globalization, technology, and specialization make persuasive communication more crucial than ever.

WHY THIS BOOK WAS WRITTEN

The thousands of participants in various business and professional speaking and writing courses I have taught want a brief summary of communication techniques. Many busy professionals have found other books on communication skills too long, insultingly remedial, or full of irrelevant information.

This book is appropriate for you if you want a guide that is short, professional, and readable.

- *Short.* The book summarizes results and models culled from thousands of pages of text and research. I have omitted bulky examples, cases, footnotes, and exercises.
- *Professional.* This book includes only information that professionals will find useful. You will not find instructions for study skills, such as in-class writing and testing; secretarial skills, such as typing letters and answering telephones; artistic skills, such as writing dialogue and performing dramatic readings; or job-seeking skills, such as résumé writing and job interviewing.
- *Readable.* I have tried to make the book clear and practical. The format makes it easy to read and to skim. The tone is direct, matter-of-fact, and nontheoretical.

HOW THIS BOOK IS ORGANIZED

The book is divided into four main sections.

Communication strategy (Chapter I)

Effective managerial communication—written or oral—is based on an effective strategy. Therefore, you should analyze the five strategic variables covered in this chapter before you start to write or speak: (1) communicator strategy (objectives, style, and credibility); (2) audience strategy (who they are, what they know, what they feel, how you can motivate them); (3) message strategy (how to emphasize and organize); (4) channel choice strategy (when to write and when to speak); and (5) culture strategy (how cultural differences affect your strategy).

Writing (Chapters II, III, IV, and appendices)

Chapter II offers techniques on the writing process, how to write more efficiently. Chapter III deals with "macro," or larger, issues in writing—including document design, coherence and emphasis, and paragraphs. Chapter IV covers "micro," or smaller, writing issues—including editing for brevity and choosing a style. The appendices cover writing formats, wording, grammar, and punctuation.

Speaking (Chapters V, VI, and VII)

The speaking section discusses three aspects of business speaking. Chapter V explains the verbal aspects, or what you say, in presentations, question-and-answer sessions, meetings, group collaborations, and other speaking situations. Chapter VI describes visual aids, both those prepared in advanced and those generated during the discussion. Chapter VII analyzes nonverbal delivery and listening skills.

Reference

The last section of the book contains appendices that deal with formats, correct words, unbiased language, grammar, and punctuation. Finally, the bibliography lists my sources. See the bibliography if you want documentation or further information about any ideas throughout the book.

ACKNOWLEDGMENTS

I offer grateful acknowledgment to the many people who helped make this book possible. First of all, my collegial family and my family of colleagues helped with ideas and revisions: Phil Anderson, Paul Argenti, Leonard and Helen-Jeanne Munter, Penny Paquette, Lindsay Rahmun, Lynn Russell, Debbie Schumann, and JoAnne Yates. Over the past twenty years, I have been privileged to work with excellent colleagues, executives, and students. My thanks to colleagues from the Managerial Communication Association and the Association for Business Communication for their research, energy, and stimulation. Thanks also to the thousands of executives from over eighty companies for their "real-world" experience and insights. I can scarcely believe that I have now taught literally thousands of students—at Dartmouth's Amos Tuck School of Business, Stanford Graduate School of Business, the International University of Japan, and the Helsinki School of Economics. To them, I offer my thanks for their challenges and ideas. Finally, I would like to point out that the bibliography on pages 191-194 lists my sources in more detail.

Mary Munter
Amos Tuck School of Business
Dartmouth College

Guide to MANAGERIAL COMMUNICATION

CHAPTER I OUTLINE

I. Communicator strategy
   1. What are your objectives?
   2. What communication style do you choose?
   3. What is your credibility?

II. Audience strategy
   1. Who are they?
   2. What do they know?
   3. What do they feel?
   4. How can you motivate them?

III. Message strategy
   1. How can you emphasize?
   2. How can you organize a strategic message?

IV. Channel choice strategy

V. Culture strategy

CHAPTER 1

Communication Strategy

Managerial communication is different from other kinds of communication. Why? Because in a business or management setting, a brilliant message alone is not sufficient: you are successful only if your message leads to the response you desire from your audience. Therefore, instead of visualizing communication as a straight line from a sender to a receiver, think of communication as a circle, as shown below, with the audience's response as one of the critical elements.

To get that desired audience response, you need to think strategically about your communication—before you start to write or speak. Strategic communication is based on five components, which you can analyze in any order: communicator (the writer or speaker) strategy, audience strategy, message strategy, channel choice strategy, and cultural context strategy.

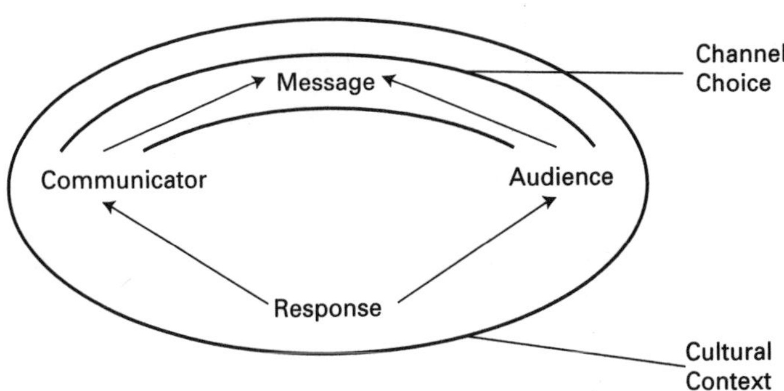

I. COMMUNICATOR STRATEGY

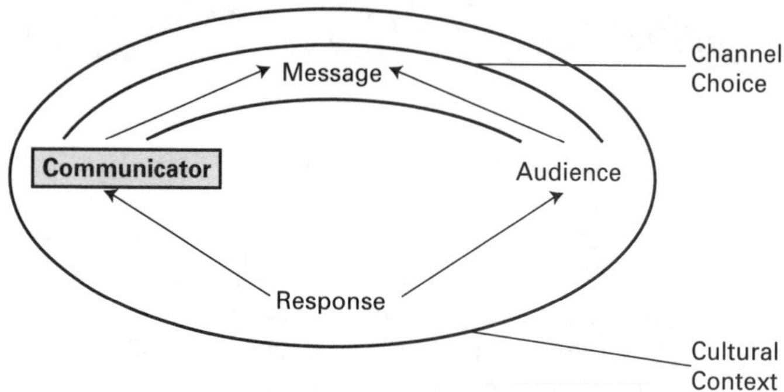

You, the communicator (writer or speaker), are clearly one of the elements in your communication strategy. This section explains how to communicate more purposefully, appropriately, and believably.

1. What are your objectives?

Defining your objectives provides two important benefits. First, you will be more efficient, because you will no longer waste time writing or presenting material unless you have a clear reason for doing so. Second, you will be more effective, because formulating your objective precisely will help you communicate more clearly. To clarify your purpose, hone your objectives from the general to the specific.

General objectives These are your broad goals, the ones that trigger the creative process and start you thinking. They are comprehensive statements about what you hope to accomplish.

Action objectives To define your objectives more specifically, determine your action objectives—specific, measurable, time-bound steps that will lead toward your general objectives. State your action objectives in this form: "To accomplish a specific result by a specific time."

Communication objective Your communication objective is even more specific. Based on your action objectives, decide precisely how you hope your audience will respond to your written or oral communication. To define your communication objective, complete this statement: "As a result of this communication, my audience will…"

EXAMPLES OF OBJECTIVES		
General	**Action**	**Communication**
Communicate departmental results.	Report X times per X time period.	As a result of this presentation, my boss will learn what my department accomplished this month.
Increase customer base.	Contract with X number of clients per X time period.	As a result of this letter, the client will sign the contract.
Develop a sound financial position.	Maintain annual debt-to-equity ratio of no greater than X.	As a result of this e-mail, the accountant will give me the pertinent information for my report. As a result of this report, the board will approve my recommendations.
Increase the number of women hired.	Hire X number by X date.	As a result of this meeting, we will come up with a strategy to accomplish our goal. As a result of this presentation, at least X number of women will sign up to interview with my firm.
Maintain market share.	See X amount by X date.	As a result of this memo, my boss will approve my marketing plan. As a result of this presentation, the sales representatives will understand our product enhancements.

2. What communication style do you choose?

Once you have defined your communication objective, choose the appropriate style to accomplish that objective. The following model (adapted from Tannenbaum and Schmidt) displays the range of communication styles used in virtually everyone's job at various times. Instead of trying to find one "right" style, use the appropriate style at the appropriate time and avoid using the same style all the time.

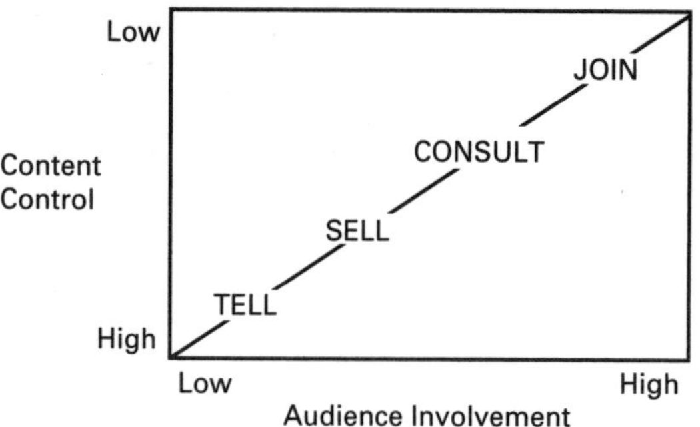

When to use the tell/sell style For the tell/sell style, you want your audience to learn from you. In the *tell* style, you are informing or explaining; as a result of the communication, you want your audience to understand something you already know. In the *sell* style, you are persuading; as a result of the communication, you want your audience to do something different. In tell/sell situations:

- You have sufficient information
- You do not need to hear others' opinions, ideas, or inputs
- You need or want to control the message content yourself

When to use the consult/join style For the consult/join style, you want to learn from the audience. The *consult* style is somewhat collaborative (like a questionnaire); the *join* style is even more collaborative (like a brainstorming session). In consult/join situations:

- You do not have sufficient information
- You need to hear others' opinions, ideas, or inputs
- You need or want to involve your audience in coming up with the message content

EXAMPLES OF OBJECTIVES AND STYLES	
Communication Objective	**Communication Style**
As a result of reading this memo, the employees will understand the benefits program available in this company. As a result of this presentation, my boss will learn what my department has accomplished this month.	**TELL:** In these situations, you are instructing or explaining. You want your audience to learn, to understand. You do not need your audience's opinions.
As a result of reading this letter, my client will sign the enclosed contract. As a result of this presentation, the committee will approve my proposed budget.	**SELL:** In these situations, you are persuading. You want your audience to do something different. You need some audience involvement to get them do so.
As a result of reading this survey, the employees will respond by answering the questionnaire. As a result of this question-and-answer session, my staff will voice and obtain replies to their concerns over the new policy.	**CONSULT:** In these situations, you are conferring. You need some give-and-take with your audience. You want to learn from them, yet control the interaction somewhat.
As a result of reading this e-mail agenda, the group will come to the meeting prepared to offer their thoughts on this issue. As a result of this brainstorming session, the group will come up with a solution to this problem.	**JOIN:** In these situations, you are collaborating. You and your audience are working together to come up with the content.

3. What is your credibility?

Another aspect of communicator strategy involves analyzing your audience's perception of you. In other words, consider your own credibility: their belief, confidence, and faith in you. Their perception of you has a tremendous impact on how you should communicate with them.

Five factors (based on the theories of French, Raven, and Kotter) affect your credibility: (1) rank, (2) goodwill, (3) expertise, (4) image, and (5) shared values. Once you understand these factors, you can enhance your credibility by stressing your initial credibility and by increasing your acquired credibility.

Initial credibility Initial credibility refers to your audience's perception of you before you even begin to communicate, before they ever read or hear what you have to say. Your initial credibility, then, may stem from their perception of who you are, what you represent, or how you have related to them previously.

As part of your communication strategy, you may want to stress or remind your audience of your initial credibility. Also, in those lucky situations in which your initial credibility is high, you may use it as a "bank account." If people in your audience regard you highly, they may trust you even in unpopular or extreme decisions or recommendations. Just as drawing on a bank account reduces your bank balance, however, drawing on your initial credibility reduces your credibility balance; you must "deposit" more to your account, perhaps by goodwill gestures or further proof of your expertise.

Acquired credibility In contrast, acquired credibility refers to your audience's perception of you after the communication has taken place, after they have read or heard what you have to say. Even if your audience knows nothing about you in advance, your good ideas and your persuasive writing or speaking will help earn you credibility. The obvious way to acquire credibility, therefore, is to do a good job of analyzing and communicating in general.

In addition, you may choose from among the techniques listed on the chart on the facing page.

FACTORS AND TECHNIQUES FOR CREDIBILITY			
Factor	**Based on**	**Initial Credibility Stress by**	**Acquired Credibility Increase by**
Rank	Hierarchical power	Emphasizing your title or rank	Associating yourself with someone of high rank (e.g., countersignature or introduction)
Goodwill	Personal relationship, "track record"	Referring to relationship or "track record"	Building goodwill by citing audience benefits
	Trustworthiness	Acknowledging conflict of interest; offering balanced evaulation	
Expertise	Knowledge, competence	Including a biography or résumé	Associating yourself with or quoting someone your audience considers expert
Image	Attractiveness, audience desire to be like you	Emphasizing attributes audience finds attractive	Building your image by identifying yourself with your audience's benefits; using nonverbals and language your audience considers dynamic
Shared values	Morality, standards	Establishing a common ground and/or your similarities, at the beginning of the communication Tying the message to your shared values	

II. AUDIENCE STRATEGY

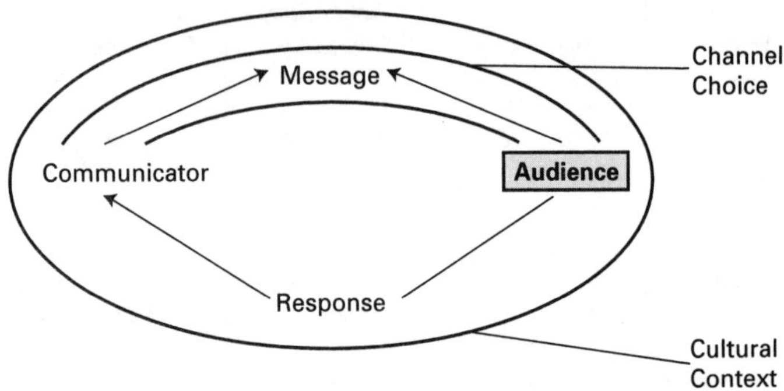

Audience strategy—that is, techniques for gearing your communication toward your audience's needs and interests—is possibly the most important aspect of your communication strategy, because it has the most effect on increasing your chances of being understood and of achieving your objective. Some communication experts recommend performing your audience analysis first; others recommend performing your communicator strategy first. All experts agree, however, that the two strategies interact with and affect one another. So, perhaps the best technique is to perform these analyses concurrently.

Audience strategy includes answering four sets of questions: (1) Who are they? (2) What do they know? (3) What do they feel? (4) How can you motivate them?

1. Who are they?

"Who are they?" sounds like a fairly straightforward question, yet choosing the people to include and focus on is often subtle and complex. To decide whom to include and how to analyze them, answer these two sets of questions.

Who should be included in your audience? In many business situations, you have, or might consider having, multiple audiences. If you are writing or speaking to more than one person, gear your message toward the person or people with the most influence over your communication objective.

- *Primary:* First of all, decide who will be included in your primary audience—who will receive your written or spoken message directly.
- *Secondary:* Consider any secondary or "hidden" audiences—those who will receive a copy of, need to approve, hear about, or be affected by your message.
- *Gatekeeper:* Is there a "gatekeeper" in your audience—someone you will need to route the message through? If so, is there any reason he or she might block your message?
- *Opinion leader:* Is there anyone in the audience who has significant informal influence?
- *Key decision-maker:* Finally, and perhaps most importantly, is there a key decision-maker, with power or influence over the outcome of the communication? If so, gear your message accordingly.

How can you find out about your audience? Once you have figured out who is or should be in your audience, analyze them as carefully as possible. Sometimes you may have market research or other data available. But much of the time audience analysis is more subjective—empathizing with or imagining you are your audience, asking the advice of someone you trust, or reflecting on your impressions.

- *As individuals:* If you can, analyze each audience member individually. Think about their educational level, training, age, sex, and interests. What are their opinions, interests, expectations, and attitudes?
- *As a group:* Even if you don't know them individually, you can analyze them as a group. What are their group characteristics? What does the group stand for? What are their shared norms, traditions, standards, rules, and values?

2. What do they know?

Based on your audience analysis, think about what they know and what they need to know in this situation. More specifically, ask yourself these three sets of questions.

How much background information do they need? What do they already know about the topic? How much jargon will they understand?

- *Low background needs:* If their background information needs are low, don't waste their time with unnecessary background or definitions.
- *High background needs:* If their background information needs are high, be sure to define new terms or jargon, link new information to information they already know, and use extremely clear structure.
- *Mixed background needs:* In some cases, you might want to review background information with an opening such as "Just to review," or put background information in a separate appendix or handout.

How much new information do they need? What do they need to learn about the topic? How much detail and evidence will they want?

- *High information needs:* If they need it, provide sufficient evidence, statistics, data, and other material.
- *Low information needs:* On the other hand, many times they don't need a lot of new information: for example, they may trust your expert opinion or delegate the decision to you. Think in terms of how much information your audience needs, not how much information you can provide.
- *Mixed information needs:* In some cases, you might want to include additional detail in a separate appendix or handout.

What are their expectations and preferences? What do they expect or prefer in terms of style, channel, or format?

- *Style preferences:* What, if anything, do they expect in terms of cultural, organizational, or personal style—such as formal or informal, straightforward or indirect, interactive or noninteractive?
- *Channel preferences:* What, if anything, do they expect in terms of channel choice—such as hard-copy documents versus electronic-mail notes or group versus individual meetings?
- *Standard length and format preferences:* What, if anything, do they expect in terms of standard length or format for documents or presentations—such as a standardized format for one-page memos with bullet points or standard half-hour weekly round-table informal meetings.

3. What do they feel?

In addition to thinking about what they know, think about what they feel. The audience's interests and biases will have a tremendous impact on your communication strategy. Answering the following sets of questions will give you a sense of the emotions your audience may be bringing to the communication.

How interested are they in your message? Is your message a high priority or low priority for your audience? How likely are they to read what you write or listen carefully to what you say? How much do they care about the issue or its outcomes? How much will the message affect their financial or organizational position, their value system, their sense of worth, their goals?

- *High interest level:* If their interest level is high, you can get right to the point without taking much time to arouse their interest. Build a good, logical argument. Do not expect a change of opinion without continued effort over time; however, if you can persuade them, their change will be more permanent than changes in a low-interest audience.
- *Low interest level:* If, on the other hand, their interest level is low, think about using a consult/join style and ask them to participate: one of the strongest ways to build support is to share control. If, however, you are using a tell/sell style, use one or more of the techniques discussed on pages 14-17 to motivate their interest. In addition, keep your message as short as possible. Long documents are intimidating, and listeners tune out what seems like rambling. Finally, for low-interest audiences, act quickly on attitude changes that may not be permanent.

What is their probable bias: positive or negative? What is their probable attitude toward your ideas or recommendations? Are they likely to favor them, be indifferent, or be opposed? What do they have to gain or lose from your ideas? Why have they not done this before? Why might they say "no"?

- *Positive or neutral:* If they are positive or neutral, reinforce their existing attitude by stating the benefits that will accrue from your message.
- *Negative:* If they are negative, try one or more of these techniques: (1) Limit your request to the smallest one possible, such as a pilot program rather than a full program. (2) Respond to anticipated objections; you will be more persuasive by stating and rejecting alternatives than having them devise their own, which they will be less likely to reject.

(3) State points you think they will agree with first; if audience members are sold on two or three key features of your proposal, they will tend to sell themselves on the other features as well. (4) Get them to agree that there is a problem, then solve the problem.

- *Liable to hear strong opposition:* Regardless of their own bias, if you think they will hear strong opposition, "inoculate" them against opposing arguments by listing them and explaining why you rejected them. If you think they will not hear strong opposition, don't bother to inoculate them.

Is your desired action easy or hard for them? As a final example of analyzing how they feel, think about whether your desired communication objective will be easy or hard for your audience to perform. Will it be time-consuming, complicated, or difficult for them?

- *Easy or hard for them:* Whether your desired action is easy or hard, always show how it supports their beliefs or benefits.
- *Hard for them:* If it is hard, try one of these techniques: (1) Break the action down into the smallest possible request, such as a signature approving an idea for someone else to implement. (2) Make the action as easy as you can, such as distributing a questionnaire they can fill in easily. (3) Provide them with a checklist they can follow easily.

4. How can you motivate them?

Based on your analysis of the knowledge and emotions your audience brings to the communication, think about how you can motivate them. Answer the question "What's in it for them?" Research on influence, persuasion, and motivation reveals a wide variety of motivational techniques. Of the following three sets of techniques, choose one or a combination that will work best for your particular audience.

Can you motivate through audience benefits? Stress any benefits your audience will gain from your message. Audience benefits can range from tangible and career benefits to ego and group benefits.

- *Tangible benefits:* What tangible benefits, if any, can you offer your audience? What can you literally give them as a part of your communication? In those rare cases in which you are in a position to offer tangible benefits, emphasize their value (e.g., profits, savings, bonuses, or product discounts) or significance as symbols (e.g., offices, furnishings, or jewelry). Most of us are not in a position to offer extravagant items in most communication situations; however, effective tangible benefits do not need to be elegant. Items such as tee-shirts, mugs, or pens will work effectively—if they are valued by the audience.
- *Career or task benefits:* (1) Sometimes you can motivate by showing how your message will enhance your audience's job—by solving a current problem, saving them time, or making their job easier or more convenient. (2) Or you can appeal to the task itself. Some audiences may appreciate the chance to be challenged or to share in tackling difficult work. They may also respond to the idea of participating in tough problem-solving or decision-making. (3) Other people respond to appeals to their career advancement or prestige. With these kinds of audiences, let them know how your message will win them organizational recognition and visibility among higher-ups, or enhance their reputation or networking contacts.
- *Ego benefits:* Some people respond to motivational devices that enhance their sense of self-worth, accomplishment, and achievement. For example, you can show them they are accepted and included by soliciting their suggestions or inviting them to participate. You can incorporate emotional support into your communication with informal verbal praise or with nonverbal smiles and nods. Or you might recognize them formally in your document, or present them with other forms of recognition, such as awards, plaques, or souvenirs.
- *Group benefits:* For audiences who value group relationships and group identity, emphasize benefits to the group as a whole: appeal to any tangible group benefits, group task enhancements, group advancements, or sense of group worth. For audiences who value solidarity with the group, use statements of group consensus or coalition rather than expert testimony or your individual credibility. For people who are very strongly influenced by the beliefs and actions of those around them, use the "bandwagon" technique. In the words of communication expert JoAnne Yates, "Although the fact that 'everyone is doing it' may not be a very good logical argument, it nevertheless influences some people."

Can you motivate through credibility? On pages 8-9, we discussed various factors that influence your credibility. Here are some techniques to apply your credibility as a motivational tool. Remember, the less your audience is involved in the topic or issue, the more important your credibility is as a motivating factor.

- *Shared-value credibility and the "common ground" technique:* One of the strongest applications of shared-value credibility is to establish a "common ground" with your audience, especially at the beginning of your communication. If you initially express opinions held in common with your audience, you will be more likely to change their opinions on other issues. Therefore, by starting from a common ground, even on an unrelated subject, you can increase your chance of persuading them of your main point. For example, refer to goals you share with your audience before focusing on your disagreement about how to achieve them.
- *Goodwill credibility and the "reciprocity" technique:* A motivational technique applying goodwill credibility is called "reciprocity" or "bargaining." People generally feel obligated to reciprocate positive actions with other positive actions and concessions with concessions. So, you might gain a favor by granting a favor; you might offer a concession to gain a concession. People feel obliged to reciprocate gifts, favors, and concessions—even uninvited or unwanted ones.
- *Rank credibility and punishment techniques:* The most extreme application of rank credibility is using threats and punishments, such as reprimands, pay cuts, demotions, or even dismissal. Although managers must use threats and punishments in certain situations, you should do so with extreme caution. Researchers have found that threats produce tension, provoke counter aggression, increase fear and dislike, work only when you're on the spot to assure compliance, and may eliminate the undesired behavior without producing the desired behavior. Therefore, threats and punishments are inappropriate for most audiences and most situations.

Can you motivate through message structure? Finally, in some situations, you might motivate your audience by the way you structure your message.

- *Opening:* Here are some ways to gain audience attention and interest at the start: (1) Use the opening to emphasize any of the benefits discussed on pages 14-15. (2) State the problem in the opening; use a problem/solution message structure. (3) Arouse their interest first, especially if it is low. (4) Begin with how the topic relates to them, especially if that relationship is not immediately apparent.
- *Body of the message:* In some situations, what you say in the body of the message can enhance your persuasiveness. (1) *The "inoculation" technique:* "Inoculate" your audience against possible opposing points of view by presenting an opposing view, then immediately refuting it. This inoculation will protect your audience from future "infection" if someone else brings up that point of view. (2) *The "foot in the door" technique:* Break the action down into the smallest possible request, one that you are likely to get (such as a pilot program), then later you will be more likely to get the larger request. Alternately, get someone to commit to a position publicly—even if he or she does not believe in it strongly. People will often become stronger supporters once they have made a public commitment. (3) *The "door in the face" technique:* The opposite of the "foot in the door" technique, the "door in the face" technique involves making an extreme request that you fully expect to be rejected, followed by a more moderate request that is then more likely to be honored. (4) *The two-sided technique:* If your audience's attitude is negative, or you believe they will hear opposing arguments, present both sides of the question. You will appear more reasonable and fair-minded. They will be more likely to reject alternatives you presented to them than alternatives they think up themselves. The more strongly your audience is likely to object, the sooner you should deal with their objections in your message structure.
- *Ending:* The message ending is another place you might use motivational techniques. Make it easy for your audience to act: for example, use a questionnaire they can fill in easily or a checklist they can follow easily; or list specific next steps or specific actions.

III. MESSAGE STRATEGY

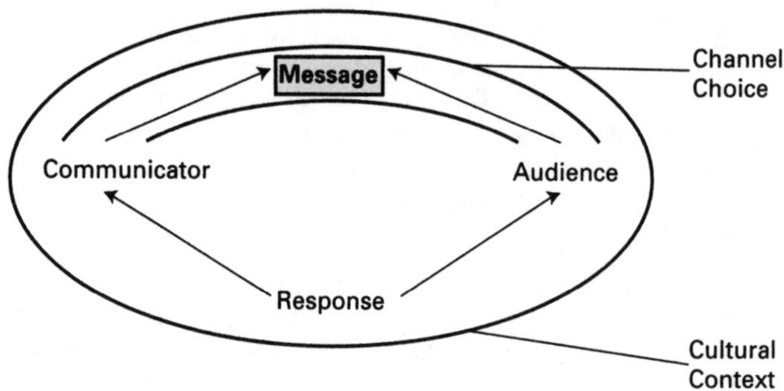

Structuring your message is a third component of your communication strategy. Unless you are working within the confines of a predetermined or standardized format, structure your message strategically for your audience. Ineffective communicators simply state their ideas in the order they happen to occur to them; effective communicators think strategically about how best to structure their message.

Instead of structuring your message as ideas happen to occur to you, then, ask the following questions: (1) How can you emphasize? (2) How can you organize?

I. How can you emphasize?

The Audience Memory Curve, illustrated below, shows what your audience is most likely to remember from your message.

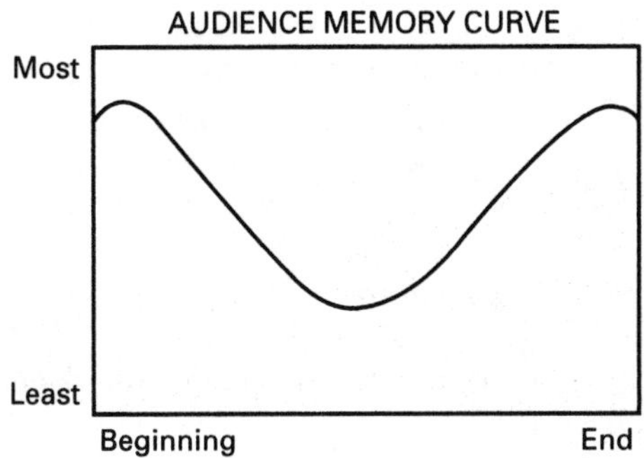

What does the Audience Memory Curve imply? First, that you should never bury important ideas in the middle. Second, that you need to keep your audience's attention throughout by using the audience appeals described on pages 14-17. Third, that your opening or introduction is extremely important. Finally, that you should state your important ideas prominently—either at the beginning or at the end (or both). Stating your main ideas first is called the direct approach; stating them last is called the indirect approach.

Using the direct approach The direct approach, stating your main ideas at the beginning of the Audience Memory Curve, is sometimes called "bottom-lining" your message because you state the bottom line first. For example:

> The committee recommends policy X for the following reasons:
>
> Reason 1
>
> Reason 2
>
> Reason 3

Advantages of the direct approach The direct approach has many advantages:

- *Improves comprehension:* People assimilate and comprehend content more easily when they know the conclusions first. Withholding your conclusion until the end is fine for a mystery story reader, but not for a busy business audience who may resent every minute they spend trying to figure out what you're getting at.
- *Is audience-centered:* The direct approach emphasizes the results of your analysis—unlike the indirect approach, which is communicator-centered because it mirrors the steps you went through to formulate your conclusions.
- *Saves time:* The direct approach saves your audience time. They can understand the message with little rereading or repetition, and they can decide immediately which sections they can skim, read carefully, or use as reference.

Why the direct approach is underutilized Why do communicators often avoid the direct approach?

- *Habit:* For one thing, communicators find it is easier to write or speak the way they think, even though it is harder on their readers or listeners.
- *Academic training:* Many communicators have been reinforced in the use of indirect structure throughout years of schooling.
- *Suspense:* Some communicators think the indirect strategy will build suspense and keep their audience's attention. In fact, it merely befuddles them.
- *Effort:* Finally, some communicators want their audience to appreciate all the effort they went through, when, in fact, such an approach may lead to unnecessary confusion rather than understanding.

When to use the direct approach Because the direct approach is easier and faster to follow, you should use it as much as possible in Anglo-American business situations, probably about 90% of the time (see pages 29-31 for cultural differences). Specifically, use the direct approach for:

- All nonsensitive messages with no emotional overtones,
- Sensitive messages if the audience's bias is positive,
- Sensitive messages if the audience is results-oriented,
- Sensitive messages if your credibility is particularly high.

Using the indirect approach An indirect approach, saving your main idea until the end of the Audience Memory Curve, involves spelling out your support first, then finishing with your generalization or conclusion. Indirect structure is sometimes called the "mystery story approach." For example,

Reason 1
Reason 2
Reason 3
Therefore, the committee recommends policy x.

When to use the indirect approach Because this approach is harder and takes longer for your audience to understand, and because it does not take advantage of the audience's attentiveness at the beginning of the message, use it only when all four of the following conditions apply:

- Sensitive message (with emotional overtones) *and*
- Your audience's bias is negative *and*
- Your audience is analysis-oriented *and*
- Your credibility is low.

Advantages of the indirect approach In the situation in which all four of these conditions apply, the indirect strategy may soften your audience's resistance, arouse their interest, and increase their tendency to see you as fair-minded. Also, the indirect approach gives you the chance to let your audience "buy into" ideas they agree with or a problem they need to solve, before you present your solution.

2. How can you organize a strategic message?

The thought process and the strategic message process are completely different. When you think, all kinds of ideas occur to you—some good, some bad, some complete, some fragmented; the end result of the thought process is your conclusion. When you form a strategic message, on the other hand, you emphasize and organize your ideas clearly for your audience. The following illustration graphically demonstrates this difference:

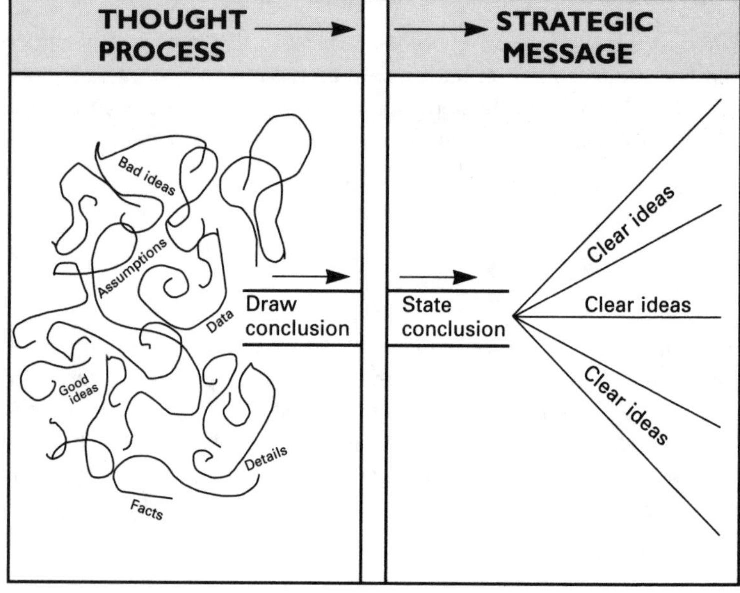

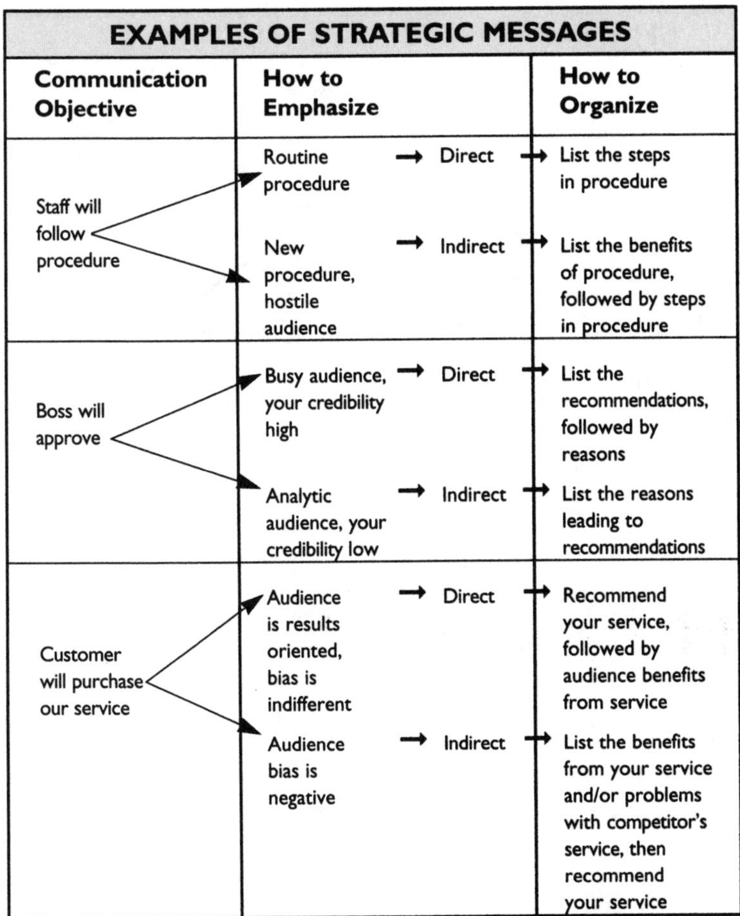

EXAMPLES OF STRATEGIC MESSAGES			
Communication Objective	**How to Emphasize**		**How to Organize**
Staff will follow procedure	Routine procedure	→ Direct	→ List the steps in procedure
	New procedure, hostile audience	→ Indirect	→ List the benefits of procedure, followed by steps in procedure
Boss will approve	Busy audience, your credibility high	→ Direct	→ List the recommendations, followed by reasons
	Analytic audience, your credibility low	→ Indirect	→ List the reasons leading to recommendations
Customer will purchase our service	Audience is results oriented, bias is indifferent	→ Direct	→ Recommend your service, followed by audience benefits from service
	Audience bias is negative	→ Indirect	→ List the benefits from your service and/or problems with competitor's service, then recommend your service

IV. CHANNEL CHOICE STRATEGY

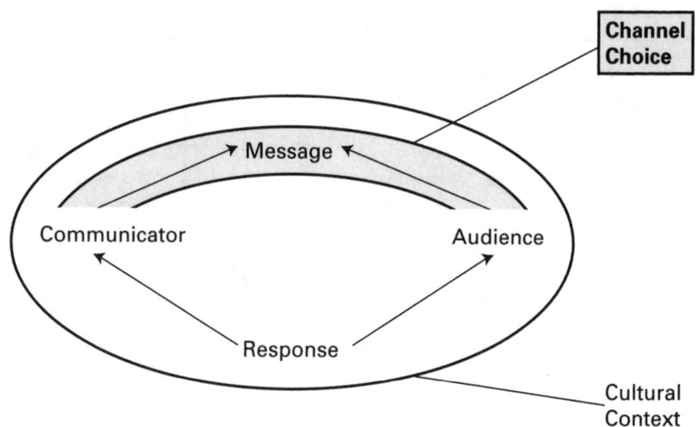

Channel choice refers to the choice of medium through which you send your message.

In the past, this strategic choice was basically between two channels: writing and speaking. Many more channels exist today—including facsimile, electronic mail, voice mail, electronic meetings, audio and video teleconferencing, electronic bulletin boards, news groups, and chat groups. These new channels sometimes change our traditional thinking about channel choice. For example, in a traditional informal meeting or chat, there is no permanent record; in an electronic meeting (where meeting participants are all simultaneously hooked together on computers or by e-mail), there is a permanent record on a print-out or a "live" board. Another example: traditional writing is usually fairly reserved, controlled, logical, and grammatically correct and does not include nonverbal cues; electronic mail, however, may be less reserved and controlled, more creative, full of grammatical and typographical mistakes, and "emoticons," such as : -), to show nonverbal cues.

Today, therefore, in addition to considering the differences between writing and speaking discussed below, your channel choice strategy should be based on your answers to the following questions.

Writing or speaking? First of all, think about the characteristics inherent in the traditional writing and speaking channels.

- *Writing* is the channel to use if you need to keep a permanent record, to get across a great deal of detail, to use precise and studied wording, or to have your audience process your message quickly (reading is faster than listening).
- *Speaking* is the channel to choose if you need a "richer" communication (it includes nonverbal cues), less rigidity and permanence, and no permanent record at this time.

Formal or informal? Writing and speaking can be either formal or informal.

- *Formal channel:* Choose a formal channel for legal negotiations or when you need to communicate key ideas and facts. Formal channels tend to be precise, controlled, technical, logical, focused, organized, informative, conclusive, decisive, action-oriented, emphatic, and forceful. Formal writing channels include most memos, proposals, reports, and letters; formal speaking channels include presentations, briefings, and lectures.
- *Informal channel:* In contrast, choose an informal channel when you need to gain new ideas from others. Informal channels tend to be fast, interactive, uninhibited, innovative, creative, open, candid, communal, and flexible. Informal channels include writing (e-mail, notes, rough drafts), speaking to a group (interactive meetings, group collaborations), and speaking to an individual (face-to-face or by voice mail).

Individual or group? Think about the relationships involved in this particular communication.

- *Individual channel:* Choose an individual channel to build an individual relationship, gain an individual response, and secure highly private and confidential matters. To reach an individual only, you might choose face-to-face discussion, desktop videoconference, telephone, voice mail, traditional writing, facsimile, or electronic mail.
- *Group channel:* On the other hand, choose a group channel to build group relationships or identity, to gain group response (including possible consensus), to avoid excluding people, or to make sure all the audience hears your message at the same time. To reach a group, choose from among presentations, questions-and-answers, electronic bulletin boards, chat groups, news groups, videoconferences, conference calls, meetings, traditional writing, facsimile, or electronic mail.

Immediate response/Control over message being received? In some situations, you need an immediate response and control over when and if your message is received. In other situations, you need neither.

- *Need immediate response:* Consider individual channels (face-to-face, desktop video, telephone) or group channels (presentations, face-to-face meetings, question and answer sessions, electronic meetings, videoconferences, conference calls).
- *Do not need immediate response:* Consider writing channels (traditional, facsimile, electronic mail) or voice mail.

Privacy or not? Another important consideration is privacy.

- *Privacy important:* Choose writing (traditional, e-mail, or facsimile—somewhat private, depending on where it's delivered), voice mail, or some forms of electronic meetings.
- *Privacy not important:* If privacy is not an issue, any group channel except electronic meetings is appropriate.

High audience participation or not? Consider how much audience participation you need.

- *High audience participation:* Choose from among one-to-one channels (phone, desktop video, face-to-face) or meeting channels (electronic, video, face-to-face).
- *Low audience participation:* Choose from among writing (traditional, facsimile, electronic mail), voice mail, or presentations (face-to-face or one-way video).

Audience in same place or not? A final consideration is the location of your audience members.

- *Geographically dispersed audience:* Choose any form of writing (traditional, facsimile, or electronic) or audio or video channels of speaking.
- *Audience in the same place:* If your audience is not dispersed, you might also choose any form of face-to-face communication (presentations, meetings, or one-to-one discussions).

The charts on the following pages summarizes various channel choice issues and trade-offs.

<table>
<tr><th colspan="4">WRITING CHANNELS</th></tr>
<tr><td>Paper</td><td>Fax
Facsimile</td><td>E-Mail
Electronic
Mail</td><td>EMS
Electronic Meeting
Systems</td></tr>
<tr><td colspan="4">Permanent and accessible record
Can reach a geographically dispersed audience
Fast for reader: reading is faster than listening
Allows for more detail: can assimilate more detail through reading than listening
Allows for more precise wording than speaking</td></tr>
<tr><td colspan="3">Low audience participation
Delayed response
No control over if or when message is received; does not interrupt receiver when received
Anonymity usually not possible</td><td>High audience participation
Immediate response
Message received immediately
Anonymity possible</td></tr>
<tr><td colspan="2">More likely to be inhibited, reserved; at best, more clear; at worst, too rigid
Usually more logical, grammatical, carefully typed
Usually takes more preparation time
Less likely to contact people in all levels of an organization
No nonverbal communication; less "rich"communication than speaking
Page shows more information than screen</td><td colspan="2">Less likely to be inhibited, reserved; at best, more creative; at worst, destructive (flaming)
Often "quick and dirty," including typos and mistakes
Usually takes less preparation time than traditional writing
More likely to contact people in all levels of an organization
Attempts to show nonverbal cues using "emoticons," such as :-) :-(
Screen shows less information than page</td></tr>
<tr><td>High privacy
Slower transmission</td><td colspan="3">May be less private than traditional writing
Faster transmission than traditional writing</td></tr>
</table>

<table>
<tr><th colspan="6">SPEAKING CHANNELS</th></tr>
<tr><th>Tell/Sell Group Presentation
Face-to-Face</th><th>Tell/Sell Group Presentation
Video or Audio</th><th>Consult/Join Meeting
Video or Face-to-Face</th><th>Consult/Join Meeting
Video or Audio</th><th>Individual
Face-to-Face</th><th>Individual
Audio</th></tr>
<tr><td colspan="6">Includes nonverbal communication
May be “richer” communication than writing
May be less rigid communication than writing
Listening takes more time than reading
Appropriate if not needed or wanted permanent record</td></tr>
<tr><td colspan="4">Can build group identity, relationships, group responses
Audience will hear the same message at the same time
Less private, less confidential
May involve more speaker preparation time</td><td colspan="2">Can build individual relationship etc.
Audience may hear differing messages, different times
Highly private and confidential
Usually less speaker preparation time
Appropriate for fast, simple answer</td></tr>
<tr><td colspan="5">Immediate response
Control if/when message received</td><td>Delayed response
No control if/when received</td></tr>
<tr><td colspan="2">Low to moderate audience participation (Q & A)</td><td colspan="3">High audience participation</td><td>Low audience participation</td></tr>
<tr><td>Audience same place</td><td>Audience may be dispersed</td><td>Audience same place</td><td>Audience may be dispersed</td><td>Audience same place</td><td>Audience may be dispersed</td></tr>
</table>

V. CULTURE STRATEGY

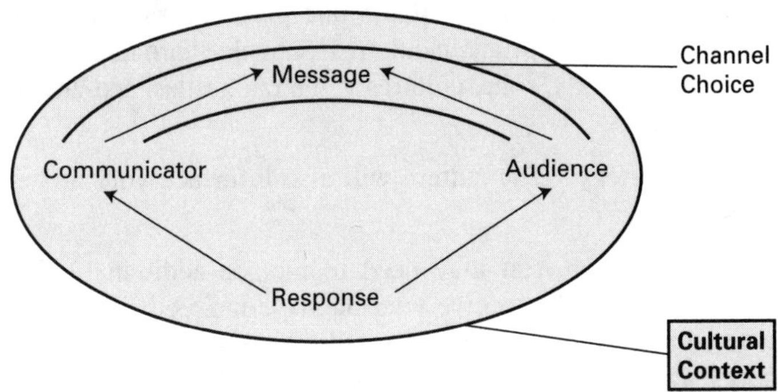

Every aspect of communication strategy we have discussed so far will be greatly influenced by the cultural context in which you are communicating. These cultural differences could result from different countries, regions, industries, organizations, genders, ethnic groups, or work groups. Keep in mind the following cultural considerations.

Communicator strategy The culture in which you communicate will affect all three aspects of communicator strategy, discussed on pages 3-9: objective, style, and credibility.

Communication objective Rethink your communication objective in terms of the culture. (1) *Time:* Consider cultural attitudes toward time: you may set a different objective in a culture that is relative, relaxed, and tradition-oriented about time than you would in a culture that is exact, precise, and future-oriented toward time. (2) *Attitude:* Think also about the cultural attitude toward fate: the objective you set in a culture believing in deterministic fate may be different from one set in a culture believing in human control over fate.

Communication style Different communication styles will tend to work better in different cultures. Group-oriented cultures may favor consult/join styles; individualistic cultures may favor tell/sell styles. Autocratic cultures may favor tell styles; democratic cultures may favor consult styles.

Credibility Different cultures place different value on the five aspects of credibility (pages 8-9). For instance, goodwill credibility is more important in cultures that value personal relations; expert credibility is more important in cultures that value hard facts and task orientation. Similarly, some cultures value rank, titles, and authority more than others.

Audience strategy The culture will also influence your audience strategy.

Audience selection You may need to include additional primary audiences (people who receive your message indirectly) and leaders (key decision-makers), depending on cultural expectations about rank, authority, and group definition. Also, remember that different cultures have different attitudes toward age, sex, and educational level.

Audience motivation Different audience motivational techniques (pages 14-17) will work more effectively in different cultures. While some cultures value material wealth and acquisition, others place greater value on work relationships, challenges, or status. Some cultures value Western logic more than others. The relative importance of individual relationships and credibility varies, as does the relative importance of group relationships and identity. Finally, values and ideals vary tremendously among cultures.

Message strategy In addition, cultural factors will influence your choice of message structure. Cultures valuing slow, ritualistic negotiations may favor indirect structures; cultures valuing fast, efficient negations may favor direct structures. Authoritarian cultures may favor direct structures downward and indirect structures upward.

Channel strategy Culture may even influence decisions regarding channel choice strategy. For example, cultures valuing personal trust more than hard facts tend to prefer oral communication and oral agreements; cultures valuing facts and efficiency tend to prefer written communication and written agreements.

Other considerations In addition to the other strategic variables we have discussed in this chapter, culture affects style, language, and nonverbal messages.

Style You may need to adjust your writing and speaking style in different cultures—for example, how politely, personally, or colorfully you write or how formally, demonstratively, or loudly you speak.

Language Language differences can affect not only denotation (word meanings) but also connotation (word implications). Even more important, differences in language may reflect differences in perception, thought processes, and forms of reasoning. Finally, consider dialects, accents, slang, jargon, and codes among different regional groups, subcultures, and professions.

Nonverbal messages Nonverbal differences present another set of challenges in cross-cultural communication.

- *Body and voice:* Consider cultural norms regarding body and voice: posture, gestures, eye contact and direction of gaze, facial expression, touching behaviors, pitch, volume, rate, and attitude toward silence. Avoid gestures considered rude or insulting in that culture; resist applying your own culture's nonverbal meanings to other cultures. For example, Vietnamese may look down to show respect, but that doesn't mean they are "shifty"; Northeasterners may speak fast, but that doesn't mean they are "arrogant."
- *Space and objects:* Also consider norms regarding space and objects: how much personal space people expect or need, how much institutional space people receive (who works where, with how much space, and with what material objects), how people dress, and how rigid dress codes are. For example, Latin Americans may prefer closer social space; the British may prefer more distant social space.
- *Greetings and hospitality:* Finally, consider cultural norms regarding greetings and hospitality: how people greet one another—handshakes, hugs, bows and so forth—and expectations regarding food and hospitality—when, where, what, and how food is prepared, presented, and eaten. Knowing these norms can go a long way toward increasing your rapport and credibility.

Once you have set your communication strategy by analyzing all five elements covered in this chapter, then do the following:

- *For writing:* Turn to chapters II, III, IV, and Appendices
- *For speaking:* Turn to chapters V, VI, and VII

COMMUNICATION STRATEGY CHECKLIST
1. Communicator Strategy (See pages 3-9.) 1. What is your communication objective: "As a result of this communication, my audience will..."? 2. What communication style do you choose: tell, sell, consult, or join? 3. What is your credibility: rank, goodwill, expertise, image, shared values?
2. Audience Strategy (See pages 10-17.) 1. Who are they: primary, secondary, gatekeeper, opinion leader(s), key decision-maker(s)? 2. How can you analyze them: as individuals? as a group? 3. What do they know: necessary background information and new information, expectations for style, channel, and format? 4. What do they feel: interest level, probable bias, hard or easy for them?
3. Message Strategy (See pages 18-23.) 1. How can you emphasize: direct or indirect? 2. How can you organize a strategic message?
4. Channel Choice Strategy (See pages 24-28.) Writing or speaking? formal or informal? immediate response needed? privacy needed? audience in same place or not? individual or group? high audience participation needed or not?
5. Culture Strategy (See pages 29-31.) 1. How does the culture affect the communicator strategy: objective, style, credibility? 2. How does the culture affect the audience strategy: selection and motivation? 3. How does the culture affect the message strategy: direct or indirect? 4. How does the culture affect the channel choice strategy?

GUIDE TO THE GUIDE TO MANAGERIAL COMMUNICATION

To set your communication strategy → See Chapter I

- Communicator strategy (objectives, style, and credibility)
- Audience strategy (selection, analysis, and motivation)
- Message strategy (emphasis and organization)
- Channel choice strategy (write or speak)
- Culture strategy (cultural variables)

If you are writing,

- To enhance the writing process → See Chapter II
  - Compose efficiently
  - Overcome writing problems
- To write effectively on macro level → See Chapter III
  - Document design
  - Coherence and emphasis
  - Paragraphs
- To write effectively on the micro level → See Chapter IV
  - Editing for brevity
  - Editing for style
- To use business formats → See Appendix A
  - Memos, reports, letters
- To write correctly → See Appendixes B-E
  - Correct words, grammar, and punctuation

If you are speaking,

- To structure what you say → See Chapter V
  - Tell/sell presentations
  - Questions and answers
  - Meetings
  - Group collaborations
  - Special situations
- To use effective visual aids → See Chapter VI
  - Visuals aid design
  - Visuals aid equipment
  - Visual aid usage
- To improve your nonverbal delivery skills → See Chapter VII
  - Delivery skills
  - Listening skills

CHAPTER II OUTLINE

I. Composing efficiently
   1. Gather information.
   2. Organize your thoughts.
   3. Focus the message.
   4. Draft the document.
   5. Edit the document.

II. Dealing with writing problems
   1. Overcoming writer's block
   2. Writing in groups

CHAPTER II

Writing: The Process

This chapter deals with the process you go through when you write, and how to make it more efficient. One of the biggest differences between business writing and other kinds of writing is time constraints. Business writers often write under severe time pressures; therefore, increasing your writing efficiency is extremely important. To do so, try some of these techniques for (1) composing efficiently and (2) dealing with the special challenges of writer's block and group writing.

THE WRITING PROCESS		
Section in this chapter:	**I. Composing Efficiently**	**II. Dealing with Writing Problems**
Goal:	To write faster, more efficiently	To overcome special writing problems

I. COMPOSING EFFICIENTLY

THE WRITING PROCESS		
Section in this chapter:	**I. Composing Efficiently**	**II. Dealing with Writing Problems**
Goal:	To write faster, more efficiently	To overcome special writing problems

Before you sit down and start writing, make some decisions and set some expectations for yourself.

- *Deciding to write:* Review your strategy, deciding whether to write or not. In some situations, making the decision not to write at all is far wiser than composing articulate prose. Before you start to write, then, think about the strengths and weaknesses of writing as a channel of communication, as explained on pages 24-28.
- *Differentiating activities:* Once you decide it is appropriate to write, you will be more efficient if you can differentiate five activities in the writing process: (1) gathering, (2) organizing, (3) focusing, (4) drafting, and (5) editing—as shown in the illustration on the next page. Each of these activities calls for different skills.
- *Expecting overlap:* At the same time that you differentiate these stages, do not expect them to occur in lockstep order. Instead, during any one of these stages, expect the writing process to be "recursive"—that is, expect to rethink, to go back, to make changes, as shown by the curved arrows on the illustration on the next page. For example, once you've focused your ideas, you may find you need to collect more information for certain topics; or, once you've completed a draft, you may discover you need to reorganize some of your ideas. If you expect this kind of continual rethinking, you will take it in stride when the need for it occurs.

1. Gather information.

As you can see in the illustration below, the first step in the writing process is to gather information. You may want to collect information by synthesizing it from a variety of sources: reading previous correspondence, files, articles, books, financial statements, or printouts; interviewing by telephone or in person; accessing information from the World Wide Web, CD-ROMs, or intranet databases. Another way to gather information is more intuitive: brainstorming (by yourself or with others), free writing (forcing yourself to write for a certain amount of time, even if it doesn't make any sense), or keeping journals or notes on the project (to jot down ideas wherever and whenever they occur to you).

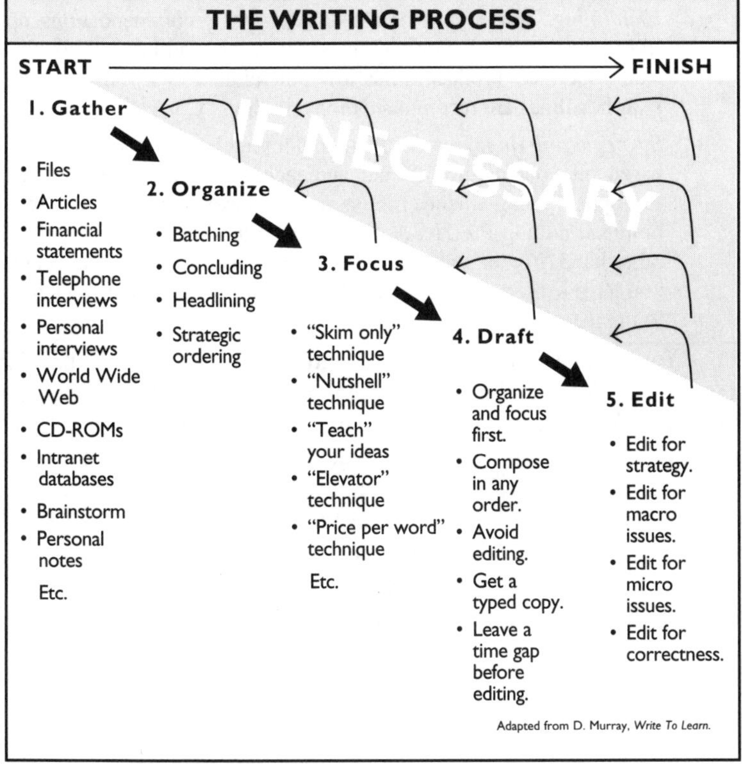

THE WRITING PROCESS
START
FINISH
IF NECESSARY
1. Gather
• Files
• Articles
• Financial statements
• Telephone interviews
• Personal interviews
• World Wide Web
• CD-ROMs
• Intranet databases
• Brainstorm
• Personal notes
Etc.
2. Organize
• Batching
• Concluding
• Headlining
• Strategic ordering
3. Focus
• "Skim only" technique
• "Nutshell" technique
• "Teach" your ideas
• "Elevator" technique
• "Price per word" technique
Etc.
4. Draft
• Organize and focus first.
• Compose in any order.
• Avoid editing.
• Get a typed copy.
• Leave a time gap before editing.
5. Edit
• Edit for strategy.
• Edit for macro issues.
• Edit for micro issues.
• Edit for correctness.

Adapted from D. Murray, *Write To Learn.*

2. Organize your thoughts.

One of the most crucial and difficult writing tasks is organizing your thoughts. You will be far more efficient if you organize before you start to draft. Admittedly, you may change your organization as you write, but you will save a lot of time in the long run if you start writing with some kind of blueprint in front of you.

Follow these four steps for organizing your ideas. Examples of these four steps are discussed on pages 40-41.

(1) *Batching:* Group similar ideas or facts together. Typical batching methods include: by examples or reasons; by time or steps in a process; by component parts; or by importance.

(2) *Concluding:* Review the batched facts, and draw conclusions or recommendations from them.

(3) *Headlining:* Move your conclusions and/or recommendations up front into a headline. For a tell message, your headlines are conclusions, such as "Product A has low potential." For a sell message, your headlines are recommendations, such as "Cut Product A."

(4) *Strategic ordering:* Decide where to put your headline (first or last), based on your credibility and audience. (See pages 18-23.) For example, if your audience is busy and you have high credibility, recommend cutting Product A, followed by the reasons why. On the other hand, if your audience is highly involved with Product A and you have low credibility, state the problems with Product A leading to the recommendation to cut it.

Your organizational blueprint might take a variety of forms: (1) a traditional linear outline, with Roman numerals, capital letters, and so forth; (2) a circular mind-map, with the main point in the middle and subordinate points drawn like spokes around the circle; (3) a sideways idea tree, with subordinate points shown growing from the side of the main point; (4) a pyramidal idea tree, as illustrated on page 43, with subordinate points displayed below the main points, or (5) any other form that works for you. (See the illustration on pages 42-43 for an example of one recommended method, called an "idea chart.")

3. Focus the message.

Now, step back from the details and try to see the essence of the message. Here are some techniques to focus your ideas.

- *Imagine the reader skimming:* Ask yourself, "What does my audience need to know most? If they only skim my message, what is the absolute minimum they should learn?"
- *"Nutshell" your ideas:* In the words of writing expert Linda Flower, "nutshell" your ideas. In a few sentences—that is, in a nutshell—lay out your main ideas. Distinguish major and minor ideas, decide how they are all related.
- *"Teach" your ideas:* Once you can express your ideas in a nutshell to yourself, think about how you would teach those ideas to someone else. Like nutshelling, trying to teach your ideas helps you form concepts in such a way that your audience gets the point, not just a list of facts.
- *Use the "elevator" technique:* Another way to focus your ideas is to imagine meeting your audience in the top floor elevator. You have only the time it takes the elevator to descend to explain your main ideas. What would you say?
- *Use the "price per word" technique:* A final technique to focus your ideas is to imagine you were paying an outrageous price per word to communicate. How would you encapsulate your main ideas to save money?

At this stage in the process, you will have an organized, focused list. For example, you might have a list of three to five steps in a procedure, examples supporting a conclusion, component parts of a process, chronological list of events, reasons why they should buy this product, or recommendations for approval. Upon analyzing this focused list, you may find you need to go back and gather additional information.

Although the writing process is recursive, be sure to complete the first three stages, generally referred to as "prewriting" (gathering, organizing, and focusing), before you start composing. Experts observe that effective writers spend about 50% of their time on prewriting activities, as opposed to drafting and editing.

EXAMPLES: GATHER INFORMATIC

I. GATHER INFORMATION

Gather a list of unrelated facts or ideas.

	Fact	Product B targets growing youth market.
Tell	Fact	Materials for Product A are in short supply.
	Fact	Competition for Product A is increasing.
or	Fact	Product B has spin-off opportunities.
Sell	Fact	Test market shows demand for Product B in Europe.
	Fact	Customer demand for Product A is decreasing.

II. ORGANIZE YOUR THOUGHTS

(1.) Batching Group similar facts or ideas together.

	Fact	Materials for Product A are in short supply.
Tell	Fact	Competition for Product A is increasing.
	Fact	Customer demand for Product A is decreasing.
or	Fact	Product B targets growing youth market.
Sell	Fact	Product B has spin-off opportunities.
	Fact	Test market shows demand for Product B in Europe.

(2.) Concluding Draw conclusions and/or recommendations.

	Fact	Materials for Product A are in short supply.	
Tell	Fact	Competition for Product A is increasing.	***Product A has low potential.***
	Fact	Customer demand for Product A is decreasing.	
or			
Sell	Fact	Product B targets growing youth market.	
	Fact	Product B has spin-off opportunities.	***Product B has high potential.***
	Fact	Test market shows demand for Product B in Europe.	

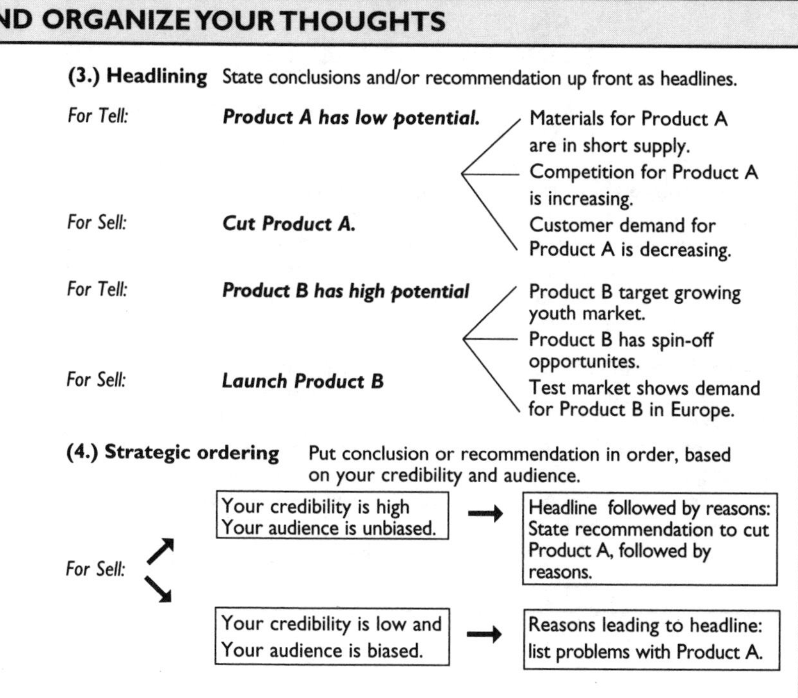
ND ORGANIZE YOUR THOUGHTS
(3.) Headlining State conclusions and/or recommendation up front as headlines.
For Tell: Product A has low potential.
For Sell: Cut Product A.
Materials for Product A are in short supply.
Competition for Product A is increasing.
Customer demand for Product A is decreasing.
For Tell: Product B has high potential
For Sell: Launch Product B
Product B target growing youth market.
Product B has spin-off opportunites.
Test market shows demand for Product B in Europe.
(4.) Strategic ordering Put conclusion or recommendation in order, based on your credibility and audience.
For Sell:
Your credibility is high Your audience is unbiased.
Headline followed by reasons: State recommendation to cut Product A, followed by reasons.
Your credibility is low and Your audience is biased.
Reasons leading to headline: list problems with Product A.

ORGANIZE YOUR THOUGHTS USING AN IDEA CHART

You may choose from among many techniques for organizing your writing: outlining, mind-mapping, drawing tree diagrams or Gantt charts, using index cards or post-its, or using computer outlining software. One useful technique is using "idea charts." Idea charts look like organizational charts, as shown in the example below. Many composition experts recommend using idea charts. Idea charts are visual, so you can literally see how parts fit together; they are flexible, so you can modify them easily; and they can actually help you come up with new ideas.

To sketch an idea chart, keep in mind three rules of thumb. First, make sure any higher-level idea generalizes about or summarizes all the lower-level ideas branching out below it. Second, check that all branches at the same level are the same kind of idea—for example, all reasons, all steps, all problems, or all recommendations. Last, limit the number of branches on your tree. Your audience's short-term working memory, their attention span, can handle only five to seven main points. Therefore, group no more than five to seven main branches on any level.

EXAMPLE: ORGANIZE YOUR THOUGHTS USING AN IDEA CHART

Unorganized list of recommendations

Eliminate Product X.

Provide *pro forma* statements.

Redefine departmental responsiblities.

Do not approach shareholders for more capital.

Expand marketing division.

Concentrate on Product Y.

Renegotiate short-term liability.

Organized list of recommendations, using idea chart

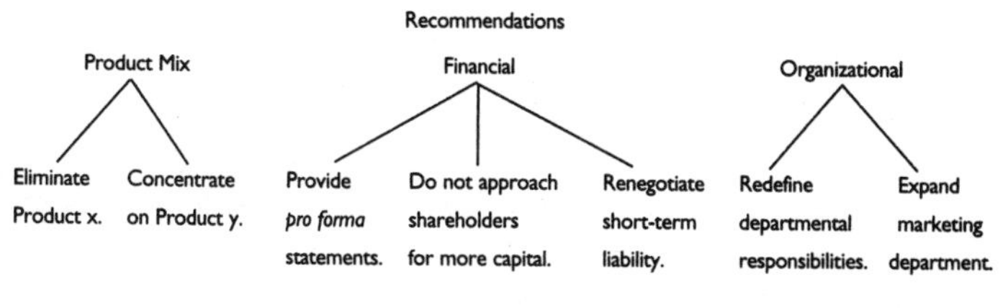

Adapted from B. Minto, *The Pyramid Prinicple.*

4. Draft the document.

The key to effective drafting is to let your creativity flow. Don't try to draft and edit at the same time. Don't be a perfectionist; don't try to write a perfect product the first time. Here are some techniques to help you in the drafting stage.

Compose in any order. Don't force yourself to write from the beginning of your document straight through to the end. Instead, write the sections you are most comfortable with first. You don't need to write your introduction first. Writing the introduction may be a formidable task, and you often end up having to change it anyway, if you modify your ideas or organization as you compose the rest of the draft. Therefore, many writing experts advise writing your introduction last.

Avoid editing. Drafting should be creative, not overly analytical. Do not worry about specific problems as you write your draft. Do not edit. If you cannot think of a word, leave a blank space; if you cannot decide between two words, write them both down. Circle or put a check mark in the margin next to awkward or unclear sections, and come back to them later.

Get typed copy. If possible, get your draft into typed copy—one side only, double-spaced, with wide margins. Most people draft faster if they avoid writing by hand: you write in longhand at about 15 words per minute; you can type at 20 to 60 words per minute; you can dictate into a machine or voice recognition software at 65 to 95 words per minute. Furthermore, most people edit faster working from typed copy. So, even if you don't type or dictate yourself, have the draft typed, preferably on a word processor.

Schedule a time gap. You will do a better job of editing if you leave some time between the creative drafting and analytical editing stages, so your thoughts can incubate subconsciously. For important or complex documents, separate the two stages by an overnight break. Even if you are under severe time constraints, or if you are composing a routine document, leave yourself a short gap: for example, begin editing after lunch or even a five- or ten-minute break.

5. Edit the document.

When you begin editing, don't immediately begin to agonize over commas and word choices. Instead, complete the four-step plan that follows to save you time by allowing you to cut or modify sections before you have wasted time perfecting them.

1. Edit for strategy. Before you begin fine-tuning, review the document for the communication strategy issues discussed in Chapter I: (1) communicator strategy (see pages 3-9), (2) audience strategy (see pages 10-17), (3) message strategy (see pages 18-23), (4) channel choice strategy (see pages 24-28), and (5) culture strategy (see pages 29-31).

2. Edit for macro issues. Before you edit at the word and sentence level, edit the document as a whole. Macroedit from a printed draft copy that allows you to see the entire document at once instead of the amount of prose you can see at one time on the display monitor. Specifically, (1) skim the document for document design (see pages 52-58); (2) read the opening, closing, and section previews only to check coherence (see pages 59-63); (3) check each paragraph or section (see pages 64-65).

3. Edit for micro issues. Once you have edited at the strategic and macro levels, then edit your sentences and words, as discussed in Chapter IV: (1) avoiding wordiness and overlong sentences (see pages 68-73) and (2) using appropriate style (see pages 74-81). In addition, check your format for consistency (see pages 164-171).

4. Edit for correctness. If you have any specific questions on wording, grammar, or punctuation, refer to the Appendices at the end of this book, pages 172-190.

Proofread carefully. Don't confuse computer proofreading for human proofreading. By all means, use computers to check spelling, punctuation, sentence length, wordiness, and grammar. However, computers cannot check for logic, flow, emphasis, tone, or computer-generated errors, such as transferring only a part of a section or not deleting a phrase you changed. Computers cannot even check all spelling errors, e.g., *you* when you meant to write *your* or *on* when you meant to write *of*. Finally, computers cannot catch missing words or phrases.

II. DEALING WITH WRITING PROBLEMS

THE WRITING PROCESS		
Section in this chapter:	**I. Composing Efficiently**	**II. Dealing with Writing Problems**
Goal:	To write faster, more efficiently	To overcome special writing problems

This section offers some ideas on how to deal with two special challenges in writing: (1) overcoming writer's block and (2) writing in collaboration with a group.

1. Overcoming writer's block

Writer's block is a temporary inability to write: you sit there facing the blank screen or the blank page and can't get the words out. Virtually everyone has experienced writer's block at one time or another. Writing is not a matter of magical inspiration that comes easily to everyone but you. If you're stuck, try one or more of these techniques.

Change the writing task. One set of techniques centers on changing the writing task you are working on at that particular moment.

- *Write another section first.* If you are stuck on one section, put it aside and write another section first. Don't force yourself to write from beginning to end. Write any section that seems easier first—even if it's the conclusion.
- *Write your headings first.* Try writing your headings, subheadings, or bullet points first. Then, go back and flesh out each one.
- *Resketch your idea chart.* Some people think more visually than verbally. If you do, sketching your idea chart, as explained on pages 42-43, can help you get going.
- *Work on non-text issues.* Work on some other part of the writing task, such as formatting or graphics, so you can have some sense of accomplishment before returning to text-writing.

Change your activity. Another set of techniques has to do with changing the kind of activity you are engaged in.

- *Take a break.* If you are bogged down with your ideas or expression, taking a break often helps. Walk away. Do something else. Allow time for the problems to incubate in your mind subconsciously. When you return after this rest period, you will often be able to work more effectively.
- *"Talk" to your reader.* Sit back and imagine that you are talking to your readers. Then, write or dictate what you would say to them. Often, wording will flow more easily and less awkwardly when you talk out loud than when you write silently.
- *Talk about your ideas.* To use this technique, talk with someone else about your writing. Discuss your ideas, or your overall organization, or specific points—whatever seems to be eluding you.
- *Read or talk about something else.* Read something else. Talk to someone about something else. Some people find that changing activities in this way allows their thoughts to develop.

Change your perceptions. A final set of techniques involves changing your perceptions about yourself and about writing.

- *Relax your commitment to rules.* Sometimes writers are blocked by what they perceive as hard-and-fast "rules," such as "Never use the word *I* in business writing." Reject these rules, especially during the drafting stage. You can always edit later on.
- *Break down the project.* Reorganize the entire writing project into a series of more manageable parts.
- *Print "draft" at the top of each page.* Print the word "draft" at the top of each page, or lightly in the background of each page, to remind yourself that you don't have to be perfect.
- *Relax your expectations.* Avoid being too self-critical. Lower unrealistic expectations for yourself. Try the relaxation techniques explained on pages 152-157.
- *Don't fall in love with your prose.* Just get something down. It doesn't have to be perfect; you may have to edit it anyway.
- *Expect complexity.* Writing is so complex that you should not expect it to go logically and smoothly, but rather to involve continual rethinking and changing. Keep in mind the illustration on page 37.

2. Writing in groups

Group writing is increasingly prevalent in business. Collaborating means compromising, but it also means benefiting from a wealth of talents and differing degrees of credibility. Here are some suggestions for writing effectively and efficiently in groups:

Agree on group guidelines. Before you start in on the writing project itself, agree on guidelines and ground rules for the group to function effectively. (See pages 98-101.) Decide who will facilitate the meetings, how you will make decisions for various items, and how you will deal with infractions of group agreements.

Agree on the tasks and timeline. Once you have agreed on general guidelines for the group, set the specific timeline and writing tasks. Sometimes, either the culture or the situation will determine who is to perform certain tasks; alternately, the group itself will decide. As you delineate the tasks and timeline, decide if and how you might use groupware—e.g., to edit various drafts of the document. Specify deadlines, yet try to build in some leeway. Finally, remember to specify what milestones you will use to identify progress and modify the timeline, if necessary. The six tasks to include on your timeline include:

Setting the strategy Agree on a time frame for, and specify who will be involved in, setting the communication strategy—communicator strategy, audience strategy, message strategy, and culture strategy—as summarized on the checklist on page 32.

Gathering information Most groups divide the research tasks based on the interests and expertise of each member. Remember to set times for periodic meetings during the research phase to pool ideas, avoid unnecessary overlap, and move together toward conclusions and recommendations.

Organizing and focusing the information Set a time to organize and focus the information, as described on pages 38-39. With group writing, it is especially important to do so extremely clearly before you start writing. Some groups organize information as a group either face-to-face or electronically; others have one person do so. Be especially sure to avoid a "data-dump" in which every bit of data submitted is poured into the final document.

Drafting the document Next on the timeline comes the drafting stage. Consider two options here:

- *Use various draft writers:* One choice is to have different people write different sections. This option is most appropriate if you want to spread the responsibility, if the writers' styles are similar, or if people want to write the section in the area of their expertise. If you use multiple draft writers, be sure to (1) agree about formality, directness, and other style issues in advance, and (2) allow enough time to edit for consistency after all the drafts are complete.
- *Use one writer:* A second option is to use one writer, who writes the entire document from scratch. This option assures you of a more consistent style throughout, avoids ownership issues with various sections, and takes advantage of a gifted writer; however, it centralizes power and responsibility with one person. If you are using one writer, be sure to (1) include him or her in the research progress meetings throughout the process, and (2) allow enough time to incorporate group revisions after the draft.

Editing the document Be sure to allow enough time for editing the document. Some groups waste time arguing about every detail of editing; others don't leave enough time to edit at all. Instead, consider these two options:

- *Use a single editor:* One choice is to use one editor—either a group member, a colleague, or a professional. If you do so, schedule enough time for him or her to edit. Agree clearly whether you want (1) a copy editor for typos, spelling, and grammar only, or (2) a style editor for consistency in style and format only, or (3) an analytic editor for strategy and content changes.
- *Use a group of editors:* A second choice is to edit as a group. Circulate hard copy or electronic copy for each group member to read and annotate. Then, (1) the group can meet face-to-face or electronically to discuss all editing issues, (2) one person can read all the comments and decide what to incorporate, or (3) the group can discuss strategy and content issues only, delegating editing for style and copyediting to one person.

Attending to final details Finally, don't forget to build into the timeline any time needed for proofreading, gaining approval of the final document if necessary, and producing and distributing the document.

CHAPTER III OUTLINE

I. Document design
   1. Using headings and subheadings
   2. Using white space
   3. Using typography

II. Coherence and emphasis
   1. In the opening and closing
   2. Throughout the document

III. Effective paragraphs

CHAPTER III

Writing: Macro Issues

The previous chapter covered methods to organize your thoughts clearly for yourself. This chapter covers methods to demonstrate that clear organization to your reader through *macro writing*, writing issues pertaining to the document as a whole. The next chapter will cover *micro writing,* writing issues pertaining to sentence and word choice.

Please note that these macro and micro issues apply equally to all kinds of written business communication, including memos, reports, and letters. See Appendix A, pages 164-171, for descriptions of these standard business formats.

MACRO WRITING			
Section in this chapter:	**I. Document Design**	**II. Coherence and Emphasis**	**III. Effective Paragraphs**
Goal:	To increase readability; to show organization	To provide logical flow	To organize paragraphs or sections
Methods:	Headings White space Typography	Openings/ Closings Throughout the document	Generalizations Topic sentences Development

I. DOCUMENT DESIGN

MACRO WRITING			
Section in this chapter:	**I. Document Design**	**II. Coherence and Emphasis**	**III. Effective Paragraphs**
Goal:	To increase readability; to show organization	To provide logical flow	To organize paragraphs or sections
Methods:	Headings White space Typography	Openings/ Closings Throughout the document	Generalizations Topic sentences Development

Many business readers will only skim your document, or only read certain sections of it carefully. Using document design techniques ensures that they will notice your important points if they do skim, and that they will be able to find sections of particular interest for more careful reading or reference. Three techniques for document design include using: (1) headings and subheadings, (2) white space, and (3) typography.

1. Using headings and subheadings

Once you have batched and headlined your ideas, as discussed on pages 37-41, translate your headlines into your headings. Effective headings and subheadings are characterized by "stand-alone sense," parallel form, and limited wording.

Stand-alone sense "Stand-alone sense" means the headings and subheadings make sense on their own, capturing the essence of your ideas. A reader should be able to read your headings and subheadings only, and understand them without reading the rest of the document.

Ineffective heading: does not make "stand-alone sense"

Recommendation

Effective heading: makes "stand-alone sense"

Recommendation: Build the new plant in Pittsburgh

Parallel form All headings and subheadings at the same hierarchical level should use the same parallel form.

Grammatical parallelism One kind of parallelism is grammatical—that is, the same grammatical construction for ideas of equal importance. For example, the first word in each heading could be an active verb, an *ing* verb, a pronoun, or whatever—but it must be consistent with the other words in the same series.

Ineffective heading: three steps are not parallel

Steps to organize internally

1. Establishing formal sale organization.
2. Production department: responsibilities defined.
3. Improve cost-accounting system.

Effective heading: three steps are parallel

Steps to organize internally

1. Establish formal sales organization.
2. Define responsibilities within the production department.
3. Improve cost-accounting system.

Conceptual parallelism "Conceptual parallelism" means that each heading should be the same kind of item.

Ineffective headings: not conceptually parallel, although grammatically parallel

Cost-Effective Optimization

- What are the options?
- What are the problems with Testing?
- What is Finite Element Analysis (FEA)?
- What are the benefits of FEA?

Effective headings: conceptually parallel

Cost Effective Optimization

- Option 1: Testing
- Option 2: FEA

2. Using white space

The term "white space" refers to empty space on the page. White space shows your organization and section breaks visually, emphasizes important ideas, and presents your ideas in more manageable bits. Readers unconsciously react favorably toward white space, so think about how you might allow for it in the following ways:

Shorter blocks of text Business readers generally do not want to see large, formidable blocks of text. A page consisting of one huge paragraph, running from margin to margin, is not as inviting or easy to read as one with shorter paragraphs and more white space. Therefore, keep most of your paragraphs short, averaging not more than 150-200 words, five sentences, or 1½ inches of single-spaced typing. On the other hand, the page will look monotonous if all the paragraphs are the same length, so vary the length of your paragraphs.

Ineffective use of white space: paragraph too long

If you consistently write very long paragraphs, your reader may just look at the page and say, "Forget it! Why should I wade through all the material to pick out the important points?" And why should your reader do that work? Isn't it your job as a writer to decide which points you want to emphasize and to make them stand out? You may want to show the creative gushing process you go through as a writer and just go on and on writing as ideas come into your head. Your psychologist, your friends, or your family might possibly be very interested in how this process works. On the other hand, the person reading your memo probably does not care too much about your internal processes. The business reader wants to see your main ideas quickly and to have the work of sorting out done for him or her. Didn't you find that just the look of this paragraph rather put you off? Did it make you want to read on? Or did it make you want to give up?

Effective use of white space and paragraph length

Medium-sized paragraphs or sections are easier for your reader to comprehend if you:

- have a general topic sentence or heading at the beginning,
- include support sentences that amplify that generalization,
- use bullet points like these if you want to show a list.

Indentations Sometimes you can use white space to show the relationships among your sections—by indenting increasingly subordinate information to the right or by setting off your opening and closing.

Example: Using indentation to show headings versus subheadings

FIRST MAIN HEADING

This section is not indented. It is typed flush with the left margin. smsnsbbsjvlreovrkio vjaikrh vaohdb

First Subheading

Here is the first subsection. Note that the entire subsection is indented. woshp nrkhqei jkbpire

Second Subheading

jdn qplsms neonbfo enr eoj dsnla eow jf ejfefef fnnenfef nfe nfw qfw fwfefe mpq

SECOND MAIN HEADING

Now that we are back to a main heading, we type flush with the left margin again. kdm nfhv eh cidh lsp

Example: Using indentation to show opening and closing

This paragraph is the opening for a short document. dk fjh tyfhg dbmo dlpwld oepsl mskej lokun gtfre

- First heading: vne lkdh nvoeo qjs m kal qpo eiuvms me nsklo fjrhwni sops lwiudhccc
- Second heading: mf dkkj gnt tju fffle ee mddd sws wskfn eee ijtrh jgiqqbf dhgik asngk jfngkf
- Third heading: relq kbgfasf gnkfdh nn hj knlgf lkgl nglnl te jgh ehgrfqa hrh grgr

The reader can easily see that this paragraph, once again flush to the left margin, is the closing.

Effective margins Normally, set margins at 1 inch to 1½ inches: longer lines can tire the reader's eye, and shorter lines can cause choppy eye movement and awkward breaks in the text.

Generally, avoid "justified" margins—margins that end evenly on the right side of the page—because the reader's eye cannot distinguish one line from another and because variable random white spaces left between words can be very distracting and irritating to the reader. So, use justified margins only if you have desktop publishing equipment that does not leave these random spaces.

Lists Using lists is another way to increase the white space on the page and make your document easier to follow. Effective lists must be both grammatically and conceptually parallel. (See page 53.)

Using lists for emphasis Use lists only for those items you want to emphasize visually.

> *Ineffective example: no list, less white space*
>
> We have to reserve the room for the training seminar at least two weeks in advance. I'm worried about getting the facilitator confirmed by then. We also need to print up posters announcing the session. Will you take care of these arrangements? Don't forget that the poster should include the room number, too.
>
> *Effective example: uses list and white space for emphasis*
>
> I just wanted to remind you about the three arrangements you agreed to handle for the training seminar:
>
> 1. Line up the facilitator and set the seminar date.
> 2. Reserve the room by November 15.
> 3. Print up the posters (including the room number) by December 1.

Choosing numbers versus bullets Lists can begin with numbers or with bullet points. The term "bullet point" refers to large dots, asterisks, or hyphens to set off items. Use bullet points if the list is not in order of importance or in time sequence. On the other hand, use numbers if the list implies a time sequence, if the list is in order of importance, or if you will need to refer to items by number.

Indenting lists Lists are easier to read if the entire numbered or bullet-pointed section is indented.

> *Effective example: list indentation*
>
> - Here is an example of an entire bullet-pointed section in which every line is indented so the bullet point stands out on its own.
>
> *Ineffective examples: list indentation*
>
> •Here is an example of an ineffective bullet-pointed section because subsequent lines "wrap around" the bullet.
>
> •Here is another example of an ineffective bullet-pointed section because only the first line is indented.

3. Choosing typography

Typography—the use of boldface, italics, underlining, fonts, sizes, and capitals—is another important document design tool to enhance high skim value. The potential danger is overusing typography, so important ideas do not stand out. When choosing typography, think about issues of consistency and readability.

Using typography consistently Use typography for important ideas and consistent patterns.

- *For important ideas only:* Use typography only for those words and phrases you want your reader to be able to skim. Generally, this means reserving typography for headings only, not using it for random words that a reader's voice might inflect spread throughout the document. If you find yourself wanting to italicize a word or phrase mid-paragraph, that's usually a sign that you need to bring that word or phrase up front as a heading.
- *In a consistent pattern:* Set a pattern and stick to it. For example, if you start off using boldface for your main headings and underlining for your secondary headings, continue to do so throughout the document, so you don't confuse your reader's expectations.

Choosing a readable font In general, serif fonts are the easiest to read for extended text. Serif fonts are those, like the one you are reading right now, with extenders on the ends of most letters. They are usually easier to read, because these extenders give the eye more to "wrap around" and can therefore be processed more quickly. They are extremely pervasive for text in business documents.

This is a serif font.

Sans serif fonts do not have extenders on the ends of letters. They usually take the reader longer to read, because this lack of extenders gives the eye less to wrap around. These fonts are used mostly for short phrases, especially in advertisements, because of their less formal, less traditional appearance.

This is a sans serif font.

Limiting the use of capital letters Generally, limit the use of all capital letters to strings of three or four words. Upper and lower case is easier to read than all capitals; use of all capitals lose their heading effectiveness in large blocks of text.

> AVOID OVERUSING CAPS. THIS PARAGRAPH TENDS TO RUN TOGETHER BECAUSE EVERY WORD IS TYPED IN ALL CAPITAL LETTERS. NO ONE PHRASE CATCHES THE READER'S ATTENTION.

> USE CAPS APPROPRIATELY. This paragraph more clearly tells the reader to avoid all caps by using them selectively, only in the heading.

Especially avoid all capital letters in sans serif type.

> DO NOT USE A SANS SERIF FONT WITH ALL CAPITAL LETTERS, AS IN THIS EXAMPLE. THE LACK OF SIZE VARIATION WITH ALL CAPITALS AND NO SERIFS MAKES THE TEXT QUITE DIFFICULT TO READ.

> This is a serif font, with a capital letter only at the beginning of each sentence. The text is easier to read because there is more size variation; it does not all run together.

Choosing a readable size Avoid downsizing the type to the proverbial "fine print" to make something fit on the page. Generally, avoid point sizes of 9 or lower except in very short bursts; use 10-point type with caution; use 12-point type for most business documents.

> Do not use 8-point type like this for extended text.

II. COHERENCE AND EMPHASIS

MACRO WRITING			
Section in this chapter:	**I. Document Design**	**II. Coherence and Emphasis**	**III. Effective Paragraphs**
Goal:	To increase readability; to show organization	To provide logical flow	To organize paragraphs or sections
Methods:	Headings White space Typography	Openings/ Closings Throughout the document	Generalizations Topic sentences Development

Effective macro writing involves more than just document design. Effective macro writing is also coherent—that is, your ideas cohere, are "glued together" clearly, for your reader. In addition, effective macro writing is emphatic—that is, your main ideas are placed prominently, at the beginning and the end of the document (as explained on pages 18-20). By making your writing coherent, you make it easier for your reader to follow your logical flow; by making your writing emphatic, you make it easier for your reader to see your important ideas. You can use coherence and emphasis techniques in your opening and closing, and in your transitions throughout the document.

1. In the opening and closing

Since the opening and closing are the most prominent parts of your document, they are important for both coherence and emphasis.

Opening Your introduction is an important place to set up the underlying logical flow for the rest of the document. An effective introduction accomplishes three aims.

- *Build reader interest ("what exists"):* One method to build reader interest and receptivity is to refer to an existing situation, to establish a context. For example,

  As we discussed last Tuesday,

  As you know, we are currently planning for the new fiscal year.

  You may also wish to refer to ideas shared with the reader, to establish a common ground (as discussed on page 16). For example:

  We don't want to sacrifice long-term profits for short-term gains.

  We need to improve market share.

- *Explain your purpose for writing ("why write"):* Let your readers know your reason or purpose for writing—so they can read with that purpose in mind. For example:

  This report summarizes the results of our fourth-quarter sales.

  I am writing to solicit your opinion on this proposal.

- *Provide a preview ("how organized"):* Include a brief "table of contents," so your readers will be able to comprehend your writing more easily and to choose specific sections for reference, if they wish. If the document is short and organized around only one group of ideas on your idea chart (see pages 42-43), then include a preview like this one:

  This memo covers five steps in the new procedure.

  If, on the other hand, your document is long and organized around many different groups of ideas on your idea chart, then include a more explicit preview that lists your section headings, like this one:

  This report is divided into three main sections: (1) what equipment you need, (2) how to use the equipment, and (3) how to maintain the equipment.

Although an effective introduction includes each of these elements, you may present them in any order, depending on your credibility and your audience's needs, as discussed on pages 8-17.

- *Purpose or preview first:* If you have high credibility or if your audience is indifferent or likely to agree with your message, state your preview or purpose first.
- *Build reader interest first:* If you have lower credibility or are less sure of your audience's agreement, build reader interest and receptivity first.

How long should an introduction be? Long documents might include a paragraph or two for each of the three aims. Short documents, on the other hand, might open with one sentence that accomplishes all three aims:

> As you requested last Tuesday (="what exists"), I have summarized (="why write") my three objections to the new marketing plan (="how organized").

Closing The end of your document is another emphatic place in the document. One option—if you are using the direct approach and if the document is long—is to restate your main ideas; obviously, however, you don't need to reiterate your main points in a one-page memo or letter. Or, if you are using the indirect approach, state your conclusions or recommendations. Perhaps the most typical closing is to end with an "action step" or "feedback mechanism." Typical examples include:

> I'll call you next Thursday to discuss this matter.
> Please let me know if I can be of further help.
> Once I have your approval, I'll proceed with this plan.

Three pitfalls to avoid in the closing include: (1) introducing a completely new topic that might divert your reader's attention from your communication objective, (2) restating your main idea in pompous words, or (3) apologizing for or undercutting your argument at the end.

2. Throughout the document

In addition to providing coherence at the beginning and end of your document, provide coherence—or bridges—between your ideas throughout the document. Three methods for doing so include transitional words, document design techniques, and section previews.

Transitional words One way to achieve coherence throughout the document is to use transitional words or phrases. The following example illustrates achieving coherence through the transitional words "first," "second," and "third."

> *Example: using transitional words for coherence*
>
> XYZ Company should follow these recommendations to clear up its financial crisis. First, cut back drastically on labor, outside services, and manufacturing overhead expenses. Second, do not approach shareholders for more capital. Third, renegotiate short-term liabilities with the banks.

Here are some examples of the transitions used most frequently in writing:

FREQUENTLY USED TRANSITIONS

To signal	Examples
Addition or amplification	and, furthermore, besides, next, moreover, in addition, again, also, similarly, too, finally, second, subsequently, last
Contrast	but, or, nor, yet, still, however, nevertheless, on the contrary, on the other hand, conversely, although
Example	for example, for instance, such as, thus, that is
Sequence	first, second, third, next, then
Conclusion	therefore, thus, then, in conclusion, consequently, as a result, accordingly, finally
Time or place	at the same time, simultaneously, above, below, further on, so far, until now

Document design techniques Another way to achieve coherence is to use document design techniques, as discussed on pages 52-58. The following example shows the same paragraph used in the example on the facing page; in this version, however, the writer achieves coherence through document design techniques—including headings and subheadings, bullet points, indentations, and typography.

Example: using document design for coherence

Recommendations For Financial Crisis

- Cut back drastically on
  - Labor,
  - Outside services,
  - Manufacturing overhead services.
- Do not approach shareholders for more capital.
- Renegotiate short-term liabilities with the banks.

Section previews If you are writing a longer document, use section previews as a further way to enhance coherence. "Section previews" are sentences or phrases that provide a preview of the forthcoming section. The following example shows how a section preview looks at the beginning of each new section throughout a long document.

Example: using section previews for coherence

This is the introduction. It builds reader receptivity, tells your purpose for writing, and gives a preview, like this: (1) Section 1, (2) Section 2, and (3) Section 3.

Section Heading 1

The introduction to each section should also let your reader know the preview for the section, such as: This section covers the first subsection and the second subsection.

First Subsection Heading

If you had third-level headings, you would introduce them in a preview sentence or phrase here—and so on throughout your document.

III. EFFECTIVE PARAGRAPHS

MACRO WRITING			
Section in this chapter:	**I. Document Design**	**II. Coherence and Emphasis**	**III. Effective Paragraphs**
Goal:	To increase readability; to show organization	To provide logical flow	To organize paragraphs or sections
Methods:	Headings White space Typography	Openings/ Closings Throughout the document	Generalizations Topic sentences Development

A third macro issue in writing has to do with paragraphs. Good paragraphs are characterized by a generalization and support, a topic sentence or heading that states the generalization, and appropriate development.

Generalization and support Each paragraph should begin with a generalization; every single sentence in the paragraph must support that generalization. Readers may not consciously look for a generalization followed by support, but intuitively they expect to see it. If you use this technique, your readers will be able to assimilate information quickly and easily.

Effective paragraph: first sentence is a generalization for all support sentences

> This procedure consists of four steps. First, do this. Second, do that. Third, do the other. Finally, do this.

Ineffective paragraph: first sentence is not a generalization

> First, do this. Second, do that. Third, do the other. Finally, do this.

Topic sentence or heading You may state your generalization in either of two ways: for standard prose paragraphs, as a topic sentence; for sections, as a heading or subheading. Here are some examples, showing the same concept as a topic sentence, then as a heading:

Example topic sentences

The new brochures are full of major printing errors.

Three causes contributed to the problem at Plant X.

Example headings

Printing Errors in Brochure

Causes of Plant X Problems

Development Finally, each paragraph or section should be fully developed: the generalization in your topic sentence or heading must be fully supported with sufficient evidence.

Ineffective: undeveloped paragraphs

Although one-sentence paragraphs are fine when used occasionally for emphasis, if you consistently write in one-sentence paragraphs, you will find they do not develop your ideas.

One-sentence paragraphs also mean you don't group your ideas together logically.

Of course the preceding sentence belongs in a paragraph with a topic sentence about the drawbacks of one-sentence paragraphs.

Effective: developed paragraph

Consistently writing one-sentence paragraphs presents several drawbacks for your reader. First, your paragraphs will lack development. Second, your ideas will not be grouped together logically. Finally, your writting will be choppy and incoherent.

See the checklist on page 82 for a summary of the macro writing issues covered in this chapter. See the following chapter for a discussion of micro writing issues.

CHAPTER IV OUTLINE

I. Editing for brevity
   1. Avoiding wordiness
   2. Avoiding overlong sentences

II. Choosing a style
   1. Businesslike or bureaucratic?
   2. Active or passive?
   3. Jargon or no jargon?

CHAPTER IV

Writing: Micro Issues

Micro issues in writing have to do with choices about sentences and words. The chart below outlines two kinds of micro issues, covered in the two sections of this chapter. The first section, on editing for brevity, discusses micro techniques to make your writing more concise. The second section, on choosing a style, has to do with decisions to make your writing style appropriate in a given situation.

MICRO WRITING		
Section in this chapter:	**I. Editing for Brevity**	**II. Choosing a Style**
Goal:	To make writing concise	To make tone appropriate
Methods:	Avoiding wordiness Avoiding overlong sentences	Businesslike or bureaucratic? Active or passive? Jargon or no jargon?

If you have micro writing questions concerning correct wording, grammar, and punctuation, see Appendices B through E at the end of this book. See the Writing Checklists at the end of this chapter, pages 82-83, for a summary of all macro and micro writing skills.

I. EDITING FOR BREVITY

MICRO WRITING		
Section in this chapter:	I. Editing for Brevity	II. Choosing a Style
Goal:	To make writing concise	To make tone appropriate
Methods:	Avoiding wordiness Avoiding overlong sentences	Businesslike or bureaucratic? Active or passive? Jargon or no jargon?

One of the advantages of writing is that you can save your audience time—since reading is faster than listening. And, of course, business readers value saving time. Therefore, use the following techniques to make your writing more concise: (1) avoiding wordiness and (2) avoiding overlong sentences.

1. Avoiding wordiness

Avoiding wordiness never means deleting essential information to keep your document short at all costs. Choices about how much or how little information your audience needs are strategic, as explained on page 12.

Instead, avoiding wordiness means omitting unnecessary words and deadwood expressions. By trimming "you are undoubtedly aware of the fact" to "you know," you have saved your reader the trouble of processing five extra words and have communicated the same idea. If you want to avoid wordiness, watch your prepositions and your use of *be* verbs.

"To be or not to be?" Beware of linking verbs. Linking verbs do no more for the sentence than add the equivalent of an equal sign. Overusing them produces wordy, lifeless sentences. The main linking verbs are forms of the verb to *be* (including *is, was, were,* and *will be*); other linking verbs include *become, look, seem, appear, sound,* and *feel.* In grammatical terms, linking verbs are those that take a complement.

Problem #1: Overused linking verbs Try circling, or have a computer program highlight, the linking verbs in a sample of your writing, and beware if you find yourself using them in most of your sentences. You need to use these linking verbs sometimes, of course, but about 75 percent of them can be eliminated.

> *Wordy sentence: linking verb "is," 8 words total*
> Plant A is successful in terms of production.
>
> *Improved sentence: verb "produces," 4 words total*
> Plant A produces well.
>
> *Wordy phrase: linking verb "appears," 12 words total*
> There appears to be a tendency on the part of investment bankers...
>
> *Improved sentence: verb "tend," 3 words total*
> Investment bankers tend...

Problem #2: Overused impersonal openings A frequent and related wordiness problem is the "impersonal opening" formed by a *be* verb coupled with it, there, or this, resulting in it is/it was, there is/there was, or this is/this was. These six impersonal openings can usually be eliminated.

> *Wordy sentence: impersonal opening "It was," 7 words total*
> **It was** clear to the manager why...
>
> *Improved sentence: no impersonal opening, 4 words total*
> The manager knew why...
>
> *Wordy sentence: impersonal opening "There is," 6 words total*
> **There is** no more space available.
>
> *Improved sentence: no impersonal opening, 5 words total*
> No more space is available.

Watch your prepositions. Overusing prepositions—words like for, to, and of, as listed on the facing page—produces wordy sentences.

Problem #1: Overused prepositions Try circling, or having a computer program highlight, all the prepositions in a sample page of your writing. If you consistently find more than four in a sentence, you need to revise and shorten. "Of" is usually the worst offender.

> *Wordy sentence: 13 prepositions, 54 words total*
>
> Central **to** our understanding **of** the problem **of** the organizational structure **in** the XYZ division **of** the ABC Company is the chain **of** command **between** the position **of** the division vice president and the subordinate departments, because although all **of** them are **under** this office, none **of** them are directly connected **up with** it.
>
> *Improved sentence: 3 prepositions, 24 words total*
>
> The organizational problem **at** the ABC company's XYZ division is centered **in** the unclear connection **between** the division vice-president and the subordinate departments.

Problem #2: Compound prepositions In addition to avoiding overuse of prepositions, watch out for compound prepositions, such as "in order to" instead of "to." See the facing page for more examples.

> *Wordy sentence: 3 compound prepositions, 22 words total*
>
> I am writing **in order to** list the potential issues **in regard to** the Russell account **in advance of** the client visit.
>
> *Improved sentence: 0 compound prepositions, 16 words total*
>
> I am writing **about** the Russell account **to** list the potential issues before the client visit.

Problem #3: Verbs with prepositions Finally, watch out for verbs that become unnecessarily elongated with prepositions.

> *Wordy sentence: verb with preposition, 11 words total*
>
> We plan to **give consideration to** the idea at our meeting.
>
> *Improved sentence: verb alone, 9 words total*
>
> We plan to **consider** the idea at our meeting.

EXAMPLES
WATCH YOUR PREPOSITIONS

1. Do not overuse prepositions.

after	by	near	to
as	for	of	under
at	from	on	until
before	in	over	up
between	like	through	with

2. Avoid compound prepositions.

Write	*Avoid compound prepositions*
about	in regard to, with reference to, in relation to, with regard to
because	due to the fact that, for the reason that, on the grounds that
before	in advance of, prior to, previous to
for	for the period of, for the purpose of
if	in the event that
near	in the proximity of
on	on the occasion of
to	in order to, for the purpose of, so as to, with a view toward
until	until such time as
when	at the point in time, at such time, as soon as
whether	the question as to whether
with	in connection with

3. Avoid verbs with prepositions.

Write	*Avoid verb plus noun plus preposition*
analyze	perform an analysis of
assume	make assumptions about
can	be in a position to
conclude	reach a conclusion about
consider	give consideration to
decide	make a decision regarding
depends	is dependent on
examine	make an examination of
realize	come to the realization that
recommend	make a recommendation that
reduce	effect a reduction in
tend	exhibit a tendency to

2. Avoiding overlong sentences

Long, complicated sentences are harder to comprehend than shorter, simpler ones. How long is too long? One well-known readability formula recommends that sentences average 17 words. Other experts recommend 20 to 25 words. And most experts agree that you should cut sentences over 40 to 50 words. But writing is not like accounting: you cannot judge sentence length by any hard-and-fast rule. Rather, your sentence is too long anytime its length makes it confusing.

Watch out for two tendencies in particular: (1) too many main ideas in a sentence, usually signaled by using the word *and* more than once in a sentence, and (2) a hard-to-find main idea in a sentence, usually signaled by having too many piled-up phrases, parenthetical ideas, and qualifiers. If you tend to write overlong sentences, here are three solutions, moving from the least emphatic (paragraph form) to the most emphatic (bullet form).

Ineffective overlong sentence: 58 words

> Regardless of their seniority, all employees who hope to be promoted will continue their education either by enrolling in the special courses to be offered by the ABC Company, scheduled to be given on the next eight Saturdays, beginning on January 24, or by taking approved correspondence courses selected from a list available in the Staff Development Office.

Option 1: break into three sentences, using transitions

> Regardless of their seniority, all employees who hope to be promoted will continue their education in one of two ways. First, they may enroll in the special courses to be offered by the ABC Company, scheduled to be given on the next eight Saturdays, beginning on January 24. Second, they may take approved correspondence courses selected from a list available in the Staff Development Office.

Option 2: break up long sentence with internal enumeration

> Regardless of their seniority, all employees who hope to be promoted will continue their education in one of two ways: (1) they may enroll in the special courses to be offered by the ABC Company, scheduled to be given on the next eight Saturdays, beginning on January 24, or (2) they may take approved correspondence courses selected from a list available in the Staff Development Office.

Option 3: break up long sentence with bullet points

Regardless of their seniority, all employees who hope to be promoted will continue their education in one of two ways:

- They may enroll in the special courses to be offered by the ABC Company, scheduled to be given on the next eight Saturdays, beginning on January 24.
- They may take approved correspondence courses selected from a list available in the Staff Development Office.

Good sentence length, however, is more subtle than merely limiting your sentences to a constant 20 to 25 words. A lack of variety in sentence length or structure can be just as deadening as strings of long sentences, so watch out for monotonous, identically structured sentences. In addition, read your writing aloud to hear how your sentences sound; watch out for a deadly lack of rhythm or for sequences of words that no one would ever use.

II. CHOOSING A STYLE

MICRO WRITING		
Section in this chapter:	**I. Editing for Brevity**	**II. Choosing a Style**
Goal:	To make writing concise	To make tone appropriate
Methods:	Avoiding wordiness Avoiding overlong sentences	Businesslike or bureaucratic? Active or passive? Jargon or no jargon?

Micro issues involved in editing for wordiness and sentence length differ significantly from issues of style. Editing for brevity is a cognitive and, to some extent, quantifiable skill. Editing for style requires more contextual sensitivity: it is bound up in your message content, your tone, your communication objective, and your relationship with the reader.

Most of us have been taught to use and have been rewarded for using an academic style of writing. Sometimes that academic style is appropriate in business—for example, when you are writing to a group of engineers. Ineffective business writers, however, use the academic style automatically, instead of adjusting their style to the situation. Three important sets of decisions regarding style are: (1) businesslike versus bureaucratic word choice, (2) active versus passive verbs, and (3) jargon versus no jargon.

1. Businesslike or bureaucratic?

Think about your options and weigh the arguments before you choose a style to use in a given situation.

Understanding the differences Businesslike and bureaucratic styles are based on these kinds of differences.

Word and phrase length Business style uses short words and phrases, like those used in normal business conversation; bureaucratic style uses longer words and phrases.

Businesslike	*Bureaucratic*
about	pursuant to, in reference to
as you requested	pursuant to your request/our discussion
be aware	be cognizant of
get the facts	ascertain the data
here are	attached please find
if you need more help	should additional assistance be required
pay	remunerate
separately	under separate cover
until	pending determination of
use	utilize, utilization of

Pronouns and names Business style uses personal pronouns and refers to the reader and writer by name. Bureaucratic style avoids personal pronouns and avoids using the reader's and the writer's names.

Businesslike	*Bureaucratic*
I, you	one
me, reader's name	the undersigned, the aforenamed
I hope you will attend.	One would hope the vice president will attend.

Contractions Business style uses occasional contractions; bureaucratic style does not.

Businesslike	*Bureaucratic*
I won't be able to attend.	The vice president will be unable to attend.

Choosing a style There are arguments to be made for both styles.

Arguments for bureaucratic style (1) Formal phrases like "pending determination of" instead of "until" sound more important. (2) Formal phrases like "the aforementioned is attached" sound more traditional. (3) Cultural norms or audience expectations may require a bureaucratic style.

Arguments for business style (1) Bureaucratic phrases like "pending determination of" instead of "until" sound wordy and stilted. (2) Imitating the habits of business predecessors is about as sensible as writing with quill and ink instead of word processors. (3) Most business cultures and business audiences dislike stodgy, pompous, or convoluted writing styles.

Using business style If you choose to write in business style, read your writing aloud or imagine yourself saying it to someone. If you wouldn't say something because it sounds too stiff or formal, don't write it. Ask yourself, for example, if you would ever say to someone, "Per your request of today's date, enclosed please find the figures on the Nakano account." Instead, you would probably say, "Here are the figures on the Nakano account."

However, you should not simply attempt to "write the way you talk." Writing and talking are very different channels: writing is not set in a conversational context, does not give you nonverbal interaction, delays feedback, and preserves errors; talking may be more rambling, slangy, and unorganized than writing. Therefore, businesslike writing is more polished than actual conversation.

2. Active or passive?

A second stylistic choice has to do with active or passive voice. The sentence *Paul decided* is active: the active agent (Paul) comes first, the active verb (decided) second. The sentence *It was decided by Paul* is passive: the passive verb (was decided) comes first, the active agent (Paul) second. Passive sentences always include or imply action done by someone or something. Both active voice and passive voice have advantages.

When to use active voice Use active voice when you want to avoid wordiness, avoid formality, place responsibility, and save your reader time.

Use active voice to avoid wordiness. Active sentences are usually shorter because they are less wordy.

> *Active: shorter*
> Paul decided.
>
> *Passive: longer*
> It was decided by Paul.

Use active voice to avoid formality. Active sentences usually sound less formal.

> *Active: less formal*
> Paul's evident bias made it hard for him to decide fairly.
>
> *Passive: more formal*
> A fair decision was rendered difficult by Paul's evident bias.

Use active voice to place responsibility. Active sentences make it easier for the reader to figure out who performed the action.

> *Active: clear who decided*
> Paul decided to undertake a special study.
>
> *Passive: unclear who decided*
> It has been decided that a special study be undertaken.

Use active voice to save the reader time. Perhaps most important, research shows that readers can process active sentences faster than passive sentences, in part because the active sentences are shorter and clearer. In the passive example below, the reader must pause momentarily and figure out who is making the statement.

> *Passive: slower for the reader to process*
> It is stated that...
>
> *Active: faster for the reader to process*
> The Tax Code states...

When to use passive voice Since passive sentences take longer for your reader to process, use them sparingly, only when you have good reason for doing so—to deemphasize the writer, avoid responsibility, or make a transition.

Use passive voice to deemphasize the writer. The passive allows writers to remove themselves from the sentence.

> *Active: emphasizes the writer*
> I recommend...
>
> *Passive: deemphasizes the writer*
> It is recommended that...

Use passive voice to avoid responsibility. The passive allows writers to avoid placing responsibility on any one agent.

> *Active: places responsibility*
> I made a mistake.
> Lou Smith made a mistake.
>
> *Passive: avoids responsibility*
> A mistake was made.

Use passive voice occasionally for transition. Sometimes, using the passive allows you to place phrases appearing in two sentences close enough together so readers can grasp their connection more easily.

> *Active: does not connect the two sentences clearly*
> We will develop a list of tasks that will include all the projects. Each program manager will monitor his or her project.
>
> *Passive: "these projects" connects the two sentences more clearly*
> We will develop a list of tasks that will include all the projects. These projects will be monitored by each program manager.

When to use the imperative If you wish to use the active voice, but you don't want to keep repeating the word "I," try using the imperative. Imperative sentences are those that start with a verb; the subject of the sentence, you, is implied. Use the imperative for these two reasons:

Use the imperative to avoid overuse of I. The imperative starts with a verb, not with I.

> *Not imperative: repeated use of I*
>
> I recommend that you improve quality control.
>
> I recommend that you increase market share.
>
> I recommend that you lower unit cost.
>
> *Imperative: avoids repeated I*
>
> Improve quality control.
>
> Increase market share.
>
> Lower unit cost.

Use the imperative to give clear instructions. Choose the imperative when you want to give clear instructions or recommendations without sounding harsh.

> *Not imperative: unclear who is supposed to do it*
>
> Quality control should be improved.
>
> *Not imperative: "you should" may sound harsh*
>
> You should improve quality control.
>
> *Imperative: gives clear instructions or recommendation*
>
> Improve quality control.

3. Jargon or no jargon?

A third stylistic consideration is how much and what kind of jargon is appropriate in any given situation.

What is jargon? Jargon is terminology associated with your field. Every profession has its jargon. An economist might write:

> The choice of exogenous variables in relation to multicollinearity is contingent upon the deviations of certain multiple coefficients,

instead of:

> Supply determines demand.

A lawyer might write:

> This policy is used in consideration of the application therefor, copy of which application is attached hereto and made part hereof, and of the payment for said insurance on the life of the above-named insured,

instead of:

> Here is your life insurance policy.

When to use jargon When you are writing to people within your field, jargon can be appropriate. Jargon is also appropriate when it serves as a shorthand that your reader understands for a complex idea or a commonly used lengthy term. Jargon is appropriate if it saves time and words without sacrificing understanding. For example, using acronyms such as EPS, LIFO, FIFO, IRR, and ROI to readers with the necessary accounting or finance backgrounds would certainly be appropriate.

When to avoid jargon First of all, avoid jargon if it is a ponderous and wordy way of saying something simple, rather than a short way of saying something complex—for example, *fiscal expenditures* instead of *cost*, *interface with* instead of *discuss*, or *render inoperative* instead of *stop*.

Second, avoid jargon if your reader doesn't understand it, may be confused by it, or might feel excluded by it.

This habit of using jargon with readers outside your field may be symptomatic of what former *Harvard Business Review* editor David Ewing calls "pathological professionalism." He asks: "Why do the perpetrators of these verbal monstrosities, knowing the material must be read and understood by innocent people, proceed with such sinister dedication? They rejoice in the difficulty of their trade. They find psychic rewards in producing esoterica and abstruse word combinations. They revel in the fact that only a small group, an elite counterculture, knows what in hell they are trying to say. Hence, the term *pathological professionalism.*"

Chapters II, III, and IV (along with the appendices) have covered ideas for managerial writing, summarized on the checklists on the following two pages. The next three chapters will discuss managerial speaking skills.

MACRO WRITING CHECKLIST
DOCUMENT- AND PARAGRAPH-LEVEL ISSUES

1. Document Design (See pages 51-58.)

1. Are your headings and subheadings effective: stand-alone sense, parallel form, and limited wording?
2. Do you use white space effectively: blocks of text, indentations, margins, and lists?
3. Do you use typography effectively: consistent manner, readable font, limited use of capitals, readable size?

2. Coherence and Emphasis (See pages 59-63.)

1. Does your opening build reader interest, explain your purpose for writing, and provide a preview? Does your closing summarize or include action steps?
2. Does your document cohere—stick together—throughout: using transitional words, document design, and section previews?

3. Effective Paragraphs (See pages 64-65.)

Does each paragraph or section have a generalization (topic sentence or heading), followed by support for that generalization?

MICRO WRITING CHECKLIST
SENTENCE- AND WORD-LEVEL ISSUES

1. Brevity: Is Your Writing Concise? (See pages 67-73.)

1. Do you avoid wordiness (overuse of prepositions and linking verbs)?
2. Do you avoid overlong sentences?

2. Style: Is Your Tone Appropriate? (See pages 74-81.)

Have you chosen an appropriate tone: businesslike or bureaucratic? active or passive? jargon or no jargon?

3. Format: Have You Used Business Formats? (See pages 164-171.)

Have you used memo, letter, or report formats effectively?

4. Correctness (See pages 172-190.)

Have you used correct words, grammar, and punctuation?

CHAPTER V OUTLINE

I. Tell/sell presentations
   1. Structuring a presentation
   2. Working from an outline

II. Questions and answers

III. Consult/join meetings
   1. Preparation before the meeting
   2. Participation during the meeting
   3. Decision-making and follow-up

IV. Group collaborations

V. Special speaking situations

CHAPTER V

Speaking: Verbal Structure

In this chapter, we consider the verbal aspect of speaking—how to structure what you say in various group speaking situations. In Chapters VI and VII, we will look at the two other aspects of presentations: visual aids and nonverbal delivery skills.

How you structure what you say depends on the situation in which you are speaking. The chart below illustrates four kinds of group speaking situations, from the least to the most interactive: (1) tell/sell presentations, (2) questions and answers, (3) meetings, and (4) group collaborations.

SPEAKING: VERBAL STRUCTURE				
Section in this chapter:	**I. Tell/Sell Presentations**	**II. Questions and Answers**	**III. Consult/Join Meetings**	**IV. Group Collaborations**
Who speaks most:	You	You to audience	You and audience	Audience
Possible purposes:	To inform, To persuade	To answer questions	To discuss, To decide	To generate ideas

The fifth and final section covers special speaking situations, such as manuscript, impromptu, team, and media presentations.

I. TELL/SELL PRESENTATIONS

SPEAKING: VERBAL STRUCTURE				
Section in this chapter:	**I. Tell/Sell Presentations**	**II. Questions and Answers**	**III. Consult/Join Meetings**	**IV. Group Collaborations**
Who speaks most:	You	You to audience	You and audience	Audience
Possible purposes:	To inform, To persuade	To answer questions	To discuss, To decide	To generate ideas

If you are speaking to a group of people primarily to inform or persuade them, use these techniques to structure what you say.

1. Structuring a presentation

Presenting information orally differs from presenting it in writing. An effective presentation structure includes: (1) an opening, (2) a preview of the main points, (3) clearly demarcated main points, and (4) a closing.

Use an effective opening. Openings are important in all forms of communication, as we discussed with the Audience Memory Curve on pages 18-20. When you make an oral presentation, however, your opening is even more crucial than it is when you write. Unlike your readers, who decide when and where to read your document, your listeners have had the time and place imposed on them; they are likely to have other things on their minds. Therefore, speech communication experts advise using your first minute or two of a presentation for your opening.

Goals Your opening should accomplish any of the following four goals that have not already been met. (1) It should arouse your audience's interest, especially if their initial interest is low. (2) It should show how the topic relates to them, especially if that relationship isn't immediately apparent. (3) If you are unknown to the audience or have low credibility, it should establish why you're competent to talk about the subject. (4) It should give you a chance to establish rapport with your audience.

Techniques To meet these goals, consider using one or more of these techniques to compose your opening.

- *Use humor.* When most people think of an opening, they think of telling a joke. Actually, you don't necessarily have to be humorous or entertaining in your opening. Use humor only if it fits your personality and style, if it is appropriate for every member of the audience, and if it relates to the specific topic or occasion.
- *Refer to the unusual.* You might open by referring to something unusual. Examples would include a rhetorical question, a promise of what your presentation will deliver, a vivid image, a startling example or story, or an important statistic.
- *Refer to the familiar.* You might open your presentation by referring to something familiar to your audience, something they can easily relate to. Examples of this kind of opening include a reference to your audience (who they are), to the occasion (why you are there), to the relationship between the audience and the subject, or to someone or something familiar to the audience.
- *Use audience motivation techniques.* You might review the audience motivation techniques discussed on pages 14-17 for possible use in your opening.

Next, give a preview. A preview is a table of contents, an agenda, an outline of what you will be covering in your presentation. Think about the contrast between listeners and readers. Your readers can skim a document, see how long it is, and read your headings and subheadings before they start reading. Your listeners, by contrast, have no idea what you will be covering unless you tell them. One of the most common problems in business presentations is the lack of a preview. Always give an explicit preview before you begin discussing your main points.

In the most formal situations, a preview might sound like this: "In the next twenty minutes, I will discuss sales in each of three regions: the Southeast, the Far West, and the Midwest." On less formal occasions, your preview might be: "I'd like to go over the sales figures in three regions." In any situation, the point of the preview is to give your audience a skeleton view, a very general outline, of what you will be discussing.

State your main points clearly. On pages 36-43, we discussed how to organize material clearly. In addition to those general organizational principles, here are four specific techniques to apply to oral presentation structure:

Follow your preview. After your opening and preview, launch into your main points. Each main point should be exactly the same as each main point you outlined in your preview; speakers often confuse their listeners by previewing one set of points and then discussing only some of them or adding extras.

Limit your main points. Be sure to limit the number of main points you make in a presentation, since listeners cannot process as much information as readers can. Experiments in cognitive psychology show that people cannot easily comprehend more than three to five main points. Naturally, this doesn't mean that you say three things and sit down; it means that you should group your complex ideas into three to five major areas.

Use explicit transitions. When you are speaking, you need longer, more explicit transitions between major sections or subsections than when you are writing. Listeners do not stay oriented as easily as readers do; they may not remember what you are listing. Instead of using short transitions like "second" or "in addition," use longer transitions, such as "the second recommendation is" or "another benefit of this system is."

Provide internal summaries. Finally, use internal summaries to conclude each major section or subsection. Listeners may not remember information they hear only once. Here is an example of an internal summary followed by an explicit transition to the next main section: "Now that we have looked at the three elements of the marketing plan—modifying the promotion program, increasing direct mail, and eliminating the coupon program—let's turn to the financial implications of this plan."

Use an effective closing. Your audience is likely to remember your last words. So don't waste your closing saying something like "Well, that's all I have to say" or "I guess that's about it."

Instead, use a strong, obvious transitional phrase—such as "to summarize" or "in conclusion"—to introduce your closing remarks. Here are some options for effective closings:

- *Give a summary.* One effective closing is to summarize your main points. You may feel as though you're being repetitive, but this kind of reinforcement is extremely effective when explaining or instructing.
- *Refer to the opening.* Another kind of closing is to refer to the rhetorical question, promise, image, or story you used in your opening.
- *End with the action steps.* Or you might end with a call to action based on what you have presented, making the "what next?" step explicit.
- *Refer to audience benefits.* As a final example, you might close by referring to the benefits your audience will gain from following the advice in your presentation.

2. Working from an outline

Another aspect of structuring a presentation has to do with the form your notes take. Businesspeople don't have the time to memorize every presentation they make; very few business speakers must read speeches word for word. (If you do, however, see page 106 on manuscript speeches.) At the same time, business audiences expect eye contact and speaker interaction, so instead of memorizing or reading, work from an outline.

Advantages of outlines With an outline, you know you can refer to notes if necessary. However, you will avoid both the overreliance on notes caused by word-for-word manuscripts and the terror of speaking with no notes at all. You can also add notes to yourself (e.g., "stand straight!" or "show line chart here").

How to outline The purpose of your outline is to jog your memory; it is not a manuscript. You want to spend most of your time during the presentation looking at the audience, not reading. Therefore, do not write out complete sentences; instead, print very short phrases for each point or subpoint. Leave lots of white space. Use big enough lettering so that you can read your notes at arm's length.

Cards versus paper Most experts suggest writing your outline on 5-by-7- or 4-by-6-inch cards, either handwritten or printed from a computer presentation program and then taped onto cards. Cards are easier to hold and carry if you move to your visual aid or elsewhere; they allow you to add, subtract, or rearrange your material easily; they help some people force themselves to outline phrases rather than writing complete sentences. Other experts suggest regular-sized paper because cards can get shuffled and you can usually put your paper down on a table, desk, or lectern. Use the method that feels more comfortable and looks less awkward for you.

Structuring your presentation in outline form is one of the three basic components of a tell/sell presentation. See pages 110-140 for ideas on composing and using tell/sell visual aids. See pages 145-157 for techniques on rehearsal and delivery.

II. QUESTIONS AND ANSWERS

SPEAKING: VERBAL STRUCTURE				
Section in this chapter:	**I. Tell/Sell Presentations**	**II. Questions and Answers**	**III. Consult/Join Meetings**	**IV. Group Collaborations**
Who speaks most:	You	You to audience	You and audience	Audience
Possible purposes:	To inform, To persuade	To answer questions	To discuss, To decide	To generate ideas

Most presentations involve interaction between the speaker and the audience in the form of questions and answers. Dealing effectively with questions and answers involves deciding when to take questions, how to take questions, what to say if you don't know the answer, and how to answer difficult questions.

When to take questions Well before the presentation, think about when you will take questions. Then, be sure to inform your audience at the beginning of the presentation. Say, for example, "Please feel free to ask questions as they come up" or "Please hold all your questions until the end of the presentation" or "Feel free to interrupt with questions of understanding or clarification, but since we only have an hour together, please hold questions of debate or discussion until the end."

Usually, audience and cultural expectations are fairly clear: the current trend in most Anglo-American business presentations is to include questions during the presentation; sometimes, however, the norm is for a question-and-answer period at the end of the presentation. If the choice is entirely up to you, think about the following advantages and disadvantages.

Questions after the presentation If you take questions after the presentation, you will maintain control over the schedule and the flow of information. However, you risk (1) losing your audience's attention and perhaps even comprehension if they cannot interrupt with their questions, and (2) placing yourself in an awkward position if important audience members interrupt with questions after you're asked them not to. Since audiences tend to remember more material from the beginning and the end of a presentation, however, having "Q&A" last places undue emphasis on the question period. To alleviate this problem, save time for a two- to three-minute summary after the question period.

Questions during the presentation If you take questions during the presentation, the questions will be more meaningful to the questioner, the feedback will be more immediate, and your audience may listen more actively. However, questions during the presentation can upset your schedule and waste time. To alleviate these problems, (1) allow enough time for questions and (2) control digressions.

How to take questions Once you've established when to take questions, prepare yourself for how you will take them.

Prepare in advance. Prepare yourself by anticipating possible questions. Try to guess what the questions will be. Bring along extra information, perhaps even extra visual aids, to answer such questions if they come up. Another way to anticipate questions is to ask a colleague to play devil's advocate during your rehearsal.

As you prepare, try to control your attitude toward the process. Instead of going in with a defensive attitude, think of it as a compliment if your listeners are interested enough to ask for clarification, amplification, or justification.

Frequently asked questions include those of: (1) value ("Are you sure we really need this?" or "What will happen if we don't do this?"), (2) cost ("Can we do it for less?"), (3) action ("How can we do it?" or "Will this action cause new problems?"), (4) details ("What is your source?" or "Is that number correct?").

Show your understanding. When someone asks a question, listen carefully to be sure you understand it before you answer. Paraphrase or summarize complicated questions to make sure you're on the right track. If the group is large, paraphrase or repeat all questions to be sure everyone in the audience hears them. If someone asks a question you don't understand, say something like "Could you restate that? I'm afraid I don't understand the question," not "Your question isn't clear."

Stick to your objective and your organization. Answer the question, but always keep your communication objective in mind. Even if you know a lot of information for your answer, limit yourself to whatever advances your objective. Don't go off on rambling tangents. If necessary, divert the question back to your main ideas. If someone asks a question you had planned to cover later in your talk, try to answer it in a nutshell and then make it clear that you will cover it in more detail later.

Keep everyone involved. Keep the entire audience involved by calling on people from various locations in the audience and by avoiding a one-to-one conversation with a single member of the audience. When you answer, maintain eye contact with the entire audience, not just with the person who asked the question. Also, avoid ending your answer by looking right at the questioner: he or she may feel invited to ask another question.

What to say if you don't know the answer Sometimes you absolutely don't know the answer; sometimes you don't know the answer without some time to gather your thoughts.

If you don't know If you don't know the answer, say, "I don't know." Even better, suggest where the person might find the answer. Better still, offer to get the answer yourself. For example, "Off the top of my head, I don't know the sales figures for that region, but I'll look them up and have them on your desk by tomorrow morning." Never hazard a guess unless you make it extremely clear that it is only a guess.

If you need some time to think If you are momentarily stymied by a question, here are some techniques to buy you some thinking time: (1) Repeat: "You're wondering how to deal with this situation." (2) Turn around: "How would you deal with this situation?" (3) Turn outward: "How would the rest of you deal with this situation?" (4) Reflect: "Good question. Let's think about that for a moment." (5) Write: If you are using a suitable visual aid, write down the main point of the question as you think.

How to answer difficult questions Some questions are especially challenging because they are confusing, controlling, or hostile.

Confusing questions Confusing questions may be long, rambling, multifaceted, or overly global. In these cases, paraphrase the question before you answer, refocusing it to make it appropriate for your communication objective. If the questioner repeats the inappropriately long version of the question, say, "I wish we had more time so we could discuss that" or "Let's explore that in more detail after the presentation is over."

Controlling questions Some questions are not really questions; they are statements. In the case of these mini-lectures, do not feel obliged to answer or to ask "So what exactly is your question?" Instead, thank them for their comments, perhaps even paraphrasing their ideas, and then proceed with your presentation.

Another form of controlling questions are questions the audience member clearly wants to answer him- or herself or that focus on his or her interests only. In these cases, you need to decide whether you want to: (1) regain control yourself by refocusing on your communication objective or (2) change your focus midstream by turning the question back to them ("What do you think we ought to do?"). For example, if you were explaining a new procedure to a large group of employees, you would probably opt to regain control; if you were talking to a small group of important clients, you would probably choose to change focus to meet their needs.

Hostile questions People may be hostile because of lack of information; in these cases, you can influence them through facts and logic. Many times, however, they may be hostile because they feel threatened, defensive, isolated, or resentful of authority or change. Faced with a hostile question, take a deep breath, identify the hostility ("I understand you feel upset about this"), and answer the question nonemotionally and nonpersonally. Sometimes, you may be able to find a common ground ("We're both trying to do what we feel is in the customer's best interest"). Sometimes, however, you have no choice but to agree to disagree, paraphrasing both points of view clearly.

III. CONSULT/JOIN MEETINGS

SPEAKING: VERBAL STRUCTURE				
Section in this chapter:	I. Tell/Sell Presentations	II. Questions and Answers	III. Consult/Join Meetings	IV. Group Collaborations
Who speaks most:	You	You to audience	You and audience	Audience
Possible purposes:	To inform, To persuade	To answer questions	To discuss, To decide	To generate ideas

We are using the term "meetings" to refer to consult/join situations (as defined on pages 6-7), as opposed to the term "presentations" for tell/sell situations. In reality, we all know that some meetings include presentations and reports, and that some presentations turn into free-for-all discussions. However, for the purposes of explaining interactive versus presentational skills, let's assume that in a meeting you are trying to elicit group feedback rather than to present your own ideas.

Many businesspeople erroneously assume that running a meeting is easy, simple, and straightforward. Actually, meetings involve a complex and difficult set of tasks. According to negotiation expert Lindsay Rahmun, meetings are difficult because of a set of inherent contradictions that she dubs "the participant's dilemma": we expect people to be thoughtful and innovative, yet simultaneously fast and efficient; we are annoyed when people don't participate and annoyed when they talk too much; we expect people to offer their best ideas, then not get defensive when those ideas are modified or rejected; we want to hold high standards of quality and resist "groupthink," yet at the same time we call people stubborn and inflexible if they don't move with the group; we want to work with a small group for efficiency, yet with a large group for inclusiveness.

Here are some guidelines for dealing with this complex set of issues: (1) preparation before the meeting, (2) participation during the meeting, and (3) decision-making and follow-up after the meeting.

1. Preparation before the meeting

You will save yourself and the participants time if you think about your objectives, participants, and agenda in advance.

Set the objective. Always ask yourself, "Is the meeting necessary?" Meetings should be reserved for group discussion and decision making, not for routine announcements. Define the meeting objective and meeting impetus as specifically as possible, so that participants will have no doubt about its purpose; state the purpose clearly on the agenda, and restate it at the beginning of the meeting.

Select the participants. Here are three considerations for selecting participants: (1) Think about the subgroups that must be represented; at the same time, remember that it's difficult to reach a consensus with more than about eight participants. (2) Consider the hierarchical levels of participants. In general, if you want to make decisions and avoid posturing and jockeying, do not include more than two hierarchical levels of participants. (3) Consider also who should facilitate the meeting. Sometimes the person who calls the meeting chairs it. But in some cases it is more effective to have someone less dominant or less involved with the job at hand facilitate the discussion, since it's hard to listen and to talk at the same time. (See "delegating tasks," on page 98.)

Set the agenda. Organized, productive, satisfactory meetings start with an effective agenda. You may want to solicit group input on the agenda in advance. Agendas don't have to be absolutely rigid; you may revise them during the course of the meeting. But you will certainly elicit better information from people if they have your agenda in advance so that they can think of ideas before the meeting. As a general rule, distribute the agenda two or three days in advance. Thus, participants will have enough time to prepare but not enough time to lose or forget about the agenda.

Scheduling agenda items As you set your agenda, think about the meeting length and order of items. Productivity tends to drop after about two hours, or if you have too many topics to cover. Schedule a series of short meetings if the agenda requires more time. Deal with long reports by asking presenters to hand in a written report for the sake of the record but to report verbally the most important items or the items on which they want group response. Decide where you want to schedule sensitive topics on the agenda. You can save sensitive topics for the end if you think opening with major disagreements might keep the meeting from proceeding effectively. Alternatively, you can start with the most important topic, even if it is sensitive, to allow sufficient time to deal with the important topic and if you fear people won't focus on the first items if they know a big controversy is coming up.

Stating purposes for agenda items Then, for each item on the agenda, answer the following questions for the participants: (1) What is the purpose of each agenda item? Clearly differentiate items that are "for your information," "for discussion," or "for a decision." (2) What is your tentative timing for each topic? (3) Who is in charge of each item? Will you have various presenters or will you run the whole meeting yourself? (4) How should they prepare? How are they expected to contribute? Don't waste time lecturing during the meeting itself; instead, include sufficient background information with the agenda. Don't put people on the spot. Let your audience know in advance what will be expected of them—for example, "Think about the pros and cons of this proposal" or "List five ideas before the meeting."

SAMPLE AGENDA EXCERPT

Agenda item	Purpose	Time	Presenter	Preparation
Review proposal	Information	5 minutes	Joan Manager	Proposal and budget (attached)
Discuss pros and cons of proposal	Discussion	20 minutes	Bob Facilitator	Think of pros and cons

We will make a decision on this proposal next month.

2. Participation during the meeting

Facilitating a meeting demands firmness, flexibility, and a willingness not to dominate the discussion. You need to encourage people to talk, yet make sure they don't talk too much; you need to write down ideas or conclusions so you can follow up effectively, yet not get so caught up in your writing that you break the flow of the discussion. Here are some techniques to help you manage this complex set of skills.

Delegating tasks Your first task is to decide what task or tasks you are going to perform yourself, and which you will delegate to someone else.

- *Facilitator:* If you have strong feelings about the subject at hand or want to participate actively, you should consider asking someone else to facilitate the discussion. The person you choose could even be someone from a different department. If you choose to facilitate yourself, you must refrain from dominating the discussion: it's difficult to facilitate discussion while you are speaking yourself and it's difficult to listen to others' points of view when you are trying to convince them of your own.
- *Scribe:* Except in short or simple meetings, you will want to record participant comments in full view of the group and to take notes to serve as a basis for some form of permanent record. You may wish to appoint someone else to serve as the front-of-the-room scribe: (1) it's hard to listen and write at the same time and (2) it will make the meeting run faster if someone else is writing, since you can go on to discuss the next point while the scribe is still recording the previous point. (See pages 141-143 for details on recording participant comments on visuals during the meeting.) You may also want to appoint someone else or the scribe to write up minutes after the meeting, to appoint someone to check the minutes before they are distributed, and to decide who will receive a copy of the minutes.
- *Timekeeper:* You may also wish to appoint someone else to serve as timekeeper, because it's hard to concentrate on the discussion and keep your mind on the time. Going over the time limit, running off on tangents, and losing control of time can be big problems; conversely, controlling the flow too much or cutting people off can also be problems. Decide how you are going to deal with time issues. Within reason, stick to your decision or group contract on timing.

Opening and closing the meeting The meeting facilitator should do the following at the beginning and the end of the meeting:

- *Set the tone.* Get people interested, involved, and enthusiastic by means of a short introduction.
- *Start on time.* Unless cultural norms dicate otherwise, start the meeting on time. If everyone has not arrived, one technique is to designate a few open spaces near people who have agreed to bring latecomers up to date.
- *Explain the agenda.* Make sure everyone understands and agrees on the meeting's purpose, impetus, agenda, and decision-making technique. Sometimes, you may wish to open the meeting by modifying the agenda or adding discussion items, with the group, but never close the meeting by asking "Does anyone have anything else to discuss?" You may choose to post the agenda on the wall or have it available as a handout.
- *Get people to agree on ground rules.* Meetings will run much more effectively if everyone agrees explicitly on the ground rules at the outset. If you wait until someone has erred before you clarify the rules, the person will feel humiliated. If, however, you made the rules clear at the start, a brief reminder will usually work. You can either work together with the group to set up ground rules, or you can list the ground rules in advance yourself. You might even consider posting the ground rules on the wall. Examples of ground rules include: We will start and stop on time. We will not interrupt. We will stick to the agenda. We will show respect for one another and not engage in personal attacks. We will not engage in in-jokes or side conversations that will destroy group cohesiveness. We will treat all information as confidential.
- *Involve people early.* The earlier you can get participants involved in some way, the more likely they are to participate. If you are dealing with a passive or quiet group, you might think of some activity or ice-breaker that involves them early in the session. See pages 104-105 for some ideas.
- *Closing the meeting.* All your work together as a group will be wasted unless you close the meeting effectively. See pages 102-103 for details on decision-making and follow-up techniques.

During the meeting Throughout the meeting, use the following skills to encourage everybody's participation.

- *Use good listening skills.* Use the listening skills discussed on pages 158-161, especially (1) asking open-ended questions that cannot be answered "yes" or "no," such as "What are your reactions to this proposal?" (2) paraphrasing participant responses by restating verbally and in writing on charts; and (3) modeling "attending skills" that give physical attention to the speaker through effective body language.
- *Show support for every person's right to speak.* Support does not necessarily mean agreement. Instead, showing support means you hear and acknowledge each idea. In fact, you may very well end up hearing contradictory ideas. That is perfectly appropriate in a meeting; you can go back and evaluate the ideas after they are all out on the table. Responses to show support include: "That idea shows a lot of thought. What do the rest of you think?" or "Let's consider what Daniel has just recommended." Responses that do not show support include: "I disagree" or "That's wrong because..." or "That won't work, because..." Finally, encourage discussion of ideas, not of personalities.
- *Avoid dominance by any one person or subgroup.* Here are some techniques to avoid letting any one person or group dominate the discussion: (1) Talk to high-status or very verbal people privately before the meeting to ensure their cooperation. (2) Sit next to disrupters, rather than across from them, so they can't catch your eye as easily. (3) Use a firm but tactful reminder of the ground rules, such as "Wait, Martha. Remember, we agreed on no interrupting." (4) Use nonverbal methods, such as turning your body toward the person who is being interrupted or raising your hand in a "wait a minute" gesture to the person who is interrupting. (5) As a next step, try a tactful but firm interruption, such as "Excuse me, George, but we need to keep our remarks brief so everyone has a chance to talk." (6) Draw in quiet people by using a technique from pages 104-105, or going around the circle and giving each person a chance to speak to the issue, or saying something along the lines of "Let's hear from those who haven't spoken yet." (7) Give the disrupter a job to do—keep the minutes, chair a subcommittee. Often, these people are looking for some kind of status or recognition. (8) Talk privately after the meeting to people who were disruptive; avoid a direct confrontation in front of the group. Try to understand them and enlist their help in making the next meeting more productive.

- *Explain your ideas.* If you have decided that it is appropriate for the facilitator to participate in the discussion, explain your own ideas quickly. Unless you are giving a formal report during the meeting, you usually won't talk for more than a few minutes at a time. Speak only when it is appropriate. Stick to the agenda; avoid extraneous ideas. Don't bring up ideas at an inappropriate time during a meeting; for example, don't start questioning the solution all over again after the group has already decided to implement it.
- *Relate to others.* Relate to others' ideas rather than grandstanding your own. If you agree with others, you might supply supporting material such as examples, statistics, or applications of the idea. If you disagree, state your disagreements carefully by disagreeing with ideas—not with people personally. Say, for example, "That project may be very time-consuming" instead of "The project Elizabeth has proposed will take too long!" Say, "I don't understand that wording" instead of "Darcy's sentence doesn't make any sense." Disagree by saying "I'm not comfortable with..." or "What concerns me about your ideas..." instead of "I disagree with..." or "That won't work because..."
- *Don't talk too much.* We all know that one person or subgroup should not dominate the meeting discussion. Most people, however, find it hard to avoid talking, especially if they are in front of the group; the person with the greatest tendency to dominate is the meeting facilitator. To control yourself, avoid interrupting, arguing, criticizing, or over-defending; don't talk for more than a couple of minutes; ask other people to contribute; ask someone else to present background information; ask questions instead of answering them; talk with people, not to them. You have decided to work with the group interactively; therefore don't give a tell/sell presentation and don't talk too much yourself.

3. Decision-making and follow-up

Most meetings involve decision-making and follow-up as well as group participation and discussion.

Decision-making Some items on your agenda may require a decision. Choose, or have the group choose, how decisions will be made—and make it clear to the participants in advance what method you plan to use. Keep in mind that decision-making methods vary in different organizations and cultures.

By one person or majority vote These two methods are quite fast and they are effective when the decision is not particularly important to everyone in the group or when there are severe time constraints. The disadvantage of these methods, however, is that some people may feel left out, ignored, or defeated—and these people may later sabotage the implementation. On the other hand, unless they are used to being part of the decision-making process, most people do not mind serving in an advisory board capacity only, as long as you make that fact clear to them in advance.

By consensus Consensus means reaching a compromise that may not be everybody's first choice but that each person is willing to agree on and implement. Consensus involves hearing all points of view and incorporating these viewpoints into the solution, so it is time-consuming and requires group commitment to the process. Unlike majority rule, consensus is reached by discussion, not by a vote. For example, the facilitator might ask "Do you all feel comfortable with this solution?" or "Seems to me we've reached consensus around this idea. Am I right?" Consensus does not mean unanimity; every participant does not hold veto power. If one person seems to be the lone holdout for a position, say something like "Well, Fran, we understand your point clearly, but the rest of us aren't convinced of the merits of that solution. Can you live with this one instead?"

Follow-up How you end the meeting can be the most crucial element of success: all the time and effort spent on the meeting itself will be wasted if the ideas are not acted upon. At the close of the meeting, gauge the mood of the group: if issues are still unresolved, consider the need for further discussion; if issues have been resolved, don't rest on your laurels. Even if you feel bored, tired, and eager to get out of the room, or excited, exhilarated, and eager to celebrate, take the time to figure out how you are going to follow up with a permanent record and an action plan.

Permanent record Most meetings should be documented with a permanent record of some kind, usually called the "minutes," to record and communicate what occurred. The nature of the minutes will vary, given the meeting's purpose: ineffective minutes are either too detailed or too general; effective minutes include the issues discussed, the options considered, the decisions reached, and the action plan. You can write the minutes yourself or appoint someone else at the beginning of the meeting. If you are using an electronic board or "live board," you can use the printout as your permanent record.

Action plan The group should agree to an action plan—sometimes called the "what next" steps, the "take aways," or the implementation plan. Write this plan (or have the scribe write it) in full view of the group, making sure it is as specific as possible: (1) what actions are to be taken, (2) who is responsible for each action, (3) the time frame for each action, and (4) how the action will be reported back to the group. A good way to start your next meeting might be to present an update on the previous meeting's action plan.

IV. GROUP COLLABORATIONS

SPEAKING: VERBAL STRUCTURE				
Section in this chapter:	**I. Tell/Sell Presentations**	**II. Questions and Answers**	**III. Consult/Join Meetings**	**IV. Group Collaborations**
Who speaks most:	You	You to audience	You and audience	Audience
Possible purposes:	To inform, To persuade	To answer questions	To discuss, To decide	To generate ideas

The difference between a "meeting," described on the last few pages, and a "group collaboration," described on the next few pages, can be fuzzy. Generally, in a meeting you are controlling and focusing the discussion more than you are in a group collaboration. For example, in a meeting, the group might be considering a set of options; in a group collaboration, the group might be brainstorming options from scratch. The two are not mutually exclusive: you might use a group collaboration technique during a meeting, just as you might ask someone to present a short tell/sell report during a meeting.

In a collaborative session, then, use all the participation skills we discussed on pages 98-101. In addition, use the recording skills we discussed on pages 141-143. Then, use additional techniques to make the session even more collaborative. For instance, sit with the group rather than standing in front of the group. Use two scribes, instead of one, to keep the ideas flowing. Do not attempt to "prime the pump" by starting with your own ideas. Remain silent, or use one of the following techniques, until someone else starts talking. The following techniques are particularly useful if you are dealing with an apathetic group, an unresponsive group, or a group typically dominated by one person or subgroup.

Forming "buzz groups" If people don't respond to questions put to the entire group, try breaking them into small "buzz groups" of three to seven people. In a smaller group, people will almost always talk more freely and comfortably. The environment is less public and pressured, and no one individual is put on the spot. You can solicit oral or written summaries from each buzz group at the end. Buzz groups are also used for breaking down a large or complex subject; each group is assigned part of the task and reports back to the main group.

Using the "brainstorming" method Most people have heard of brainstorming sessions but do not use such sessions as effectively as they might. To be most effective, brainstorming sessions should be divided into two distinct stages: (1) During the first stage, the group agrees in advance on a time limit and the general topic. Then everyone blurts out any and every idea that comes to mind. The facilitator writes down every single idea as it is stated, usually on flipcharts or a board. Participants continue to associate freely, to follow up on ideas, and to introduce new ideas without worrying about reaching a conclusion. During the first stage, no one is allowed to criticize, evaluate, react, or decide on any ideas. (2) During the second stage, the group reviews the list of ideas, grouping related ideas and striking irrelevant ones. From this more organized list, the group can work on reaching a decision.

Using the "problem-solving" method In this process, sometimes called the "reflective-thinking model," the group (1) specifically defines the problem or opportunity; (2) analyzes the problems, looking at information, data, policies, organizational schemes, and so forth; (3) determines standards or criteria by which it will measure any solution; (4) generates various possible solutions and evaluates their feasibility and consequences; (5) weighs the options and selects the best solution; and (6) decides how to implement that solution.

Using the "nominal group" method This is an unusual but increasingly popular way of making sure that all people participate. In this procedure, the participants (1) list their ideas in writing independently, not talking with other group members, possibly before the group session; (2) compile a group list, recording one item from each person's list until all are included; (3) revise the group list to reword, combine, or avoid duplicates; (4) rank the master list independently (perhaps only the top three to five items); and (5) collate the results.

V. SPECIAL SPEAKING SITUATIONS

So far we have looked at how to structure a tell/sell presentation, a question-and-answer session, a meeting, and a group collaboration. In addition to these four standard situations, you may find yourself in other kinds of situations. This section offers some additional techniques for dealing with (1) manuscript speaking, (2) impromptu speaking, (3) team presentations, and (4) media and telecommunications.

Manuscript speaking The tell/sell presentations discussed in the first section of this chapter would be prepared but not read word for word. You may find, however, that you are occasionally called upon to speak word for word from a manuscript.

Use "spoken style." The main problem people have in writing manuscript speeches is that they use "written style" instead of "spoken style." A speech in written style may look fine on paper, but when delivered, it sounds stilted, formal, and pompous. When you write a manuscript speech, then, keep in mind four aspects of spoken style: (1) Avoid phrases no one would actually say, phrases that sound stilted or are hard to pronounce. For example, you might write, "If you were asked to do so," but you would say, "If someone asked you to do that." (2) Avoid phrases separating the subject from the verb. Your reader can easily follow this sentence: "Linda Argenti, who is currently the president of ABC Company, will be the first speaker on the panel." You make it much easier for the listener, however, if you do not separate the subject from the verb: "President Linda Argenti will be the first speaker on the panel." (3) Use shorter sentences. Speech writing generally uses shorter sentences and sometimes even sentence fragments. (4) Rhythm is much more important in spoken style than in written style. Consider, for example, the rhythmic impact of Patrick Henry's famous quotation "Give me liberty or give me death." Similarly, John Kennedy's rhythmic "Ask not what your country can do for you; ask what you can do for your country" is more effective than the unrhythmic "Don't ask what your country can do for you but what you can do for it."

Write and edit. Keeping these four considerations in mind, write the first draft of your speech, or write notes and then record yourself speaking from those notes. The transcript of what you just recorded becomes the draft of the speech. Once you have a draft, edit it and then read it aloud (or have the person for whom you're writing the speech read it aloud). After making any necessary changes, you are ready to type the manuscript in its final form.

Prepare the manuscript. A speech manuscript looks different from a regular page of writing. For one thing, it should be typed in large print: some typewriters have orator or presenter typefaces; some computers will print out extra-bold or extra-large letters. The margins also look strange: leave about one third of the right side of the page blank for notes; leave about one third at the bottom of the page blank so that your head will not drop too low as you read. Since it is awkward to read a sentence that starts on one page and finishes on the next, never break a sentence between two pages. In fact, many speech experts suggest never breaking even a paragraph between two pages. Never staple the pages of a speech; the speaker should be able to slide the page to one side. Finally, many speakers underline key words for vocal emphasis.

Impromptu speaking When you speak on an impromptu basis, you talk on the spur of the moment, without advance preparation. For example, your boss may suddenly ask you to "bring us up to date on a certain service." Usually, of course, you will not be asked to make impromptu remarks unless you have some knowledge in the area.

Here are some suggestions to help you in impromptu speaking situations: (1) Anticipate. Try to avoid truly impromptu situations. Guess at the probability of your being called on during discussions, meetings, or interviews. Guess at the topics you might be asked to discuss. (2) Keep your remarks short. Say what you have to say and then stop. Do not ramble on, feeling that you must deliver a lengthy lecture. (3) Organize as well as you can. If you have a few seconds, jot down your main points. Stick to them; avoid tangents. (4) Relate to experience. You will speak more easily and confidently if you try to relate the topic to your specific experiences and to the topics you know best.

Team presentations Make sure your team presentations are organized, unified, and coherent—not simply an unrelated series of individual presentations.

Organize as a whole. The major problem with team presentations occurs when each presenter prepares a separate part, and the parts never coalesce into a coherent whole. To avoid this problem, structure your presentation agenda by content areas, not by the number of team members. After your agenda is decided, then decide who will speak when; one speaker may cover two content sections, or one content section may be covered by multiple speakers.

Provide content transitions between speakers. To begin, one team member should provide the opening and preview for the presentation as a whole. (See pages 86-88.) Between each speaker, provide an internal summary ("Now that I have explained our proposal") and a content link to the next section ("Karla will show you the financial implications of the proposal").

Use visual aids consistently. Your visuals should look alike: use the same graphic software, template, and color-coding (e.g., blue for all the main headings throughout). Your use of visuals should also be consistent in the way you use assistance, pile, discard, and meter. (See pages 138-140.)

Rehearse and deliver as a group. In a dry-run rehearsal, practice what you will say, the exact wording of your transitions, and rough drafts of your visuals. In a full-dress rehearsal, work to perfect your delivery and flow. During the presentation, remember that every member of the team is always "on stage" to the audience, from the moment you walk in the room. Be sure to look fully attentive when other group members are speaking.

Answer questions consistently. Decide beforehand how you will handle questions and answers, including such issues as who will serve as moderator to direct questions and whether you will stand or sit to answer questions. (See pages 91-93 for more on questions.)

Media and telecommunications Here are three sets of suggestions for dealing with speaking situations involving media and telecommunications.

Preparing in advance Gather your data in advance: get together any reports, correspondence, and notes you will need for reference. Also, jot down a brief outline of the points you want to cover. This will help you avoid rambling and forgetting important points or questions. If you are appearing on television or radio, anticipate questions you may be asked. Just as important, prepare the main points you want to emphasize.

Using audio devices Audio devices include telephones and microphones (for radio, television, video, or videoteleconferencing). (1) Speak conversationally, using pauses and inflection, as though you were addressing a small group of people. (2) Watch your volume and distance: omnidirectional microphones will pick up sounds equally from all directions; for unidirectional microphones, you must keep your distance (which can vary from 2 to 20 inches) constant. (3) Avoid unwanted sounds: breathe quietly; avoid rattling your paper, drumming your fingers, scraping your chair, and jingling coins.

Being on camera You will work with a camera when you are speaking on video, videoteleconferencing, or television. (1) Prepare for mechanical distractions. Rehearse on set to learn cues and see the equipment. (2) Decide where to focus: at the camera, at the interviewer, or at the other people present. If you are recording a one-person video, you will probably look directly at the camera; if you are appearing on a talk show, you will probably look at the host; if you are appearing on a videoteleconference, you will probably look at the other participants. (3) Dress appropriately. In general, dress unobtrusively, especially if you are appearing on television. Generally, that means solid colors like gray, blue, and beige. Avoid tweeds, stripes, and patterns that will appear to jump around on the screen. Avoid white, which may glare, and black, which absorbs light. Other than a watch or a wedding ring, avoid jewelry, especially if it is jangling or otherwise distracting.

CHAPTER VI OUTLINE

I. Designing the presentation as a whole
   1. List your main ideas on an agenda chart.
   2. Provide evidence on "back-up" charts.
   3. Use "message titles" and "stand-alone sense."
   4. Provide transition between each visual.

II. Designing each individual chart
   1. Designing graphs to show quantitative data
   2. Designing diagrams to show nonquantitative concepts
   3. Designing word charts to show main ideas
   4. Using typography effectively
   5. Using color effectively
   6. Editing each chart

III. Choosing visual aid equipment

IV. Using visual aids effectively
   1. Using visuals prepared in advance
   2. Facilitating group discussions with visuals

CHAPTER VI

Speaking: Visual Aids

No matter how well you have prepared what you are going to say (Chapter V) or how skilled you may be in your nonverbal speaking delivery (Chapter VII), your audience still has the capacity to daydream: they can think faster than you can speak. To keep them concentrating on your ideas, provide visual aids that back up what you're saying. Visual aids increase your audience's comprehension and retention; add interest, variety, and impact; and remain in the memory longer than words.

Here are some techniques to use for: (1) designing the visual presentation as a whole, (2) designing each individual chart, (3) choosing the equipment, and (4) using visuals effectively.

VISUAL AIDS			
I. Designing the presentation as a whole	II. Designing each individual chart	III. Choosing visual aid equipment	IV. Using visual aids effectively

I. DESIGNING THE PRESENTATION AS A WHOLE

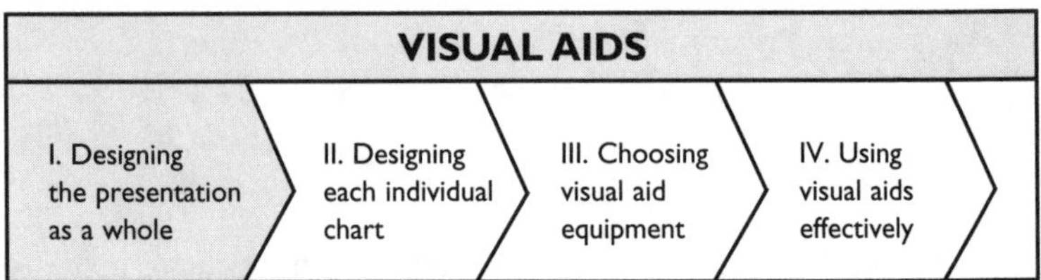

This section explains a four-step process for designing visuals to clarify your presentation structure for a tell/sell presentation as a whole. Think through the four issues in this section first, before you start the detailed process of designing individual charts, described in Section II.

1. List your main ideas on an agenda chart.

The "agenda" chart—sometimes called the "outline" or "preview" chart—forms the backbone of your presentation. The agenda slide serves as a presentation's "table of contents"; the rest of the visuals in the presentation are like the chapters amplifying the ideas in this table of contents. Therefore, plan your agenda chart carefully and make sure all your subsequent charts follow from, and relate back to, the agenda.

Example: agenda chart

Improve Growth and Efficiency for Bard Company

1. Target younger customers.
2. Consolidate operations.
3. Change product mix.

2. Provide evidence on "back-up" visuals.

The rest of the charts in your presentation are your support, or "back up," visuals. Support each section in your agenda with a series of back-up slides. Back-up slides may be graphs or diagrams (as described in more detail on pages 118-125) or word charts (as described in more detail on pages 126-129).

Example: graphical "back-up" chart

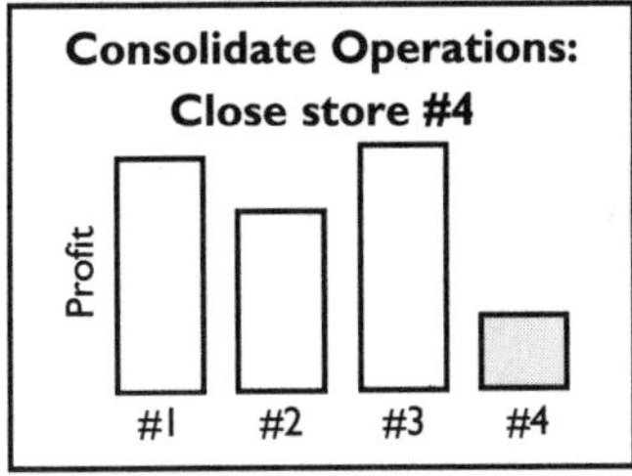

Example: word "back-up" chart

Target Younger Customers

- Pursue couples for engagement and wedding rings.
- Attract high-school students for class rings.
- Target parents of teens for graduation gifts.

3. Use "message titles" and "stand-alone sense."

Each visual should make sense to someone seeing it for the first time. Put yourself in the shoes of someone who arrived in the middle of your presentation or who missed your presentation and is reading copies of the visuals only. Two methods to increase your audience's ability to understand your visuals are "message titles" and "stand-alone sense."

Using effective message titles Use the headline at the top of each visual to reinforce the main concept in the visual. If you have a point you are trying to make in your visual, then use a *message title*—a short phrase or sentence with a point to it. Message titles are appropriate for most business presentations because usually you have a conclusion or recommendation to make. If, on the other hand, you do not have a point you are trying to make in your visual, use a *topic title*—that is, a generic phrase or generic term. Topic titles are appropriate only when you don't care what conclusion your audience draws from the data on your visual. Topic titles are easier to write than message titles, in part because they appear automatically on some computer software packages, so be sure to use them only to present uninterpreted data.

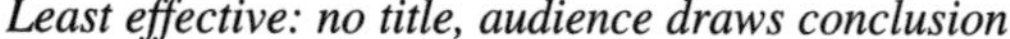

Least effective: no title, audience draws conclusion

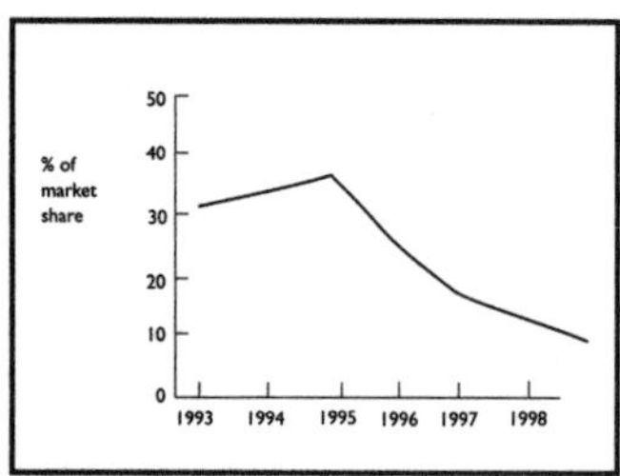

Topic title: audience draws conclusions

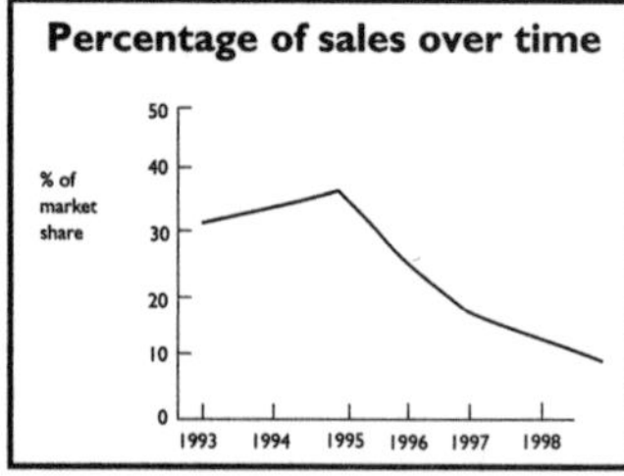

Most effective: message title, speaker draws conclusion

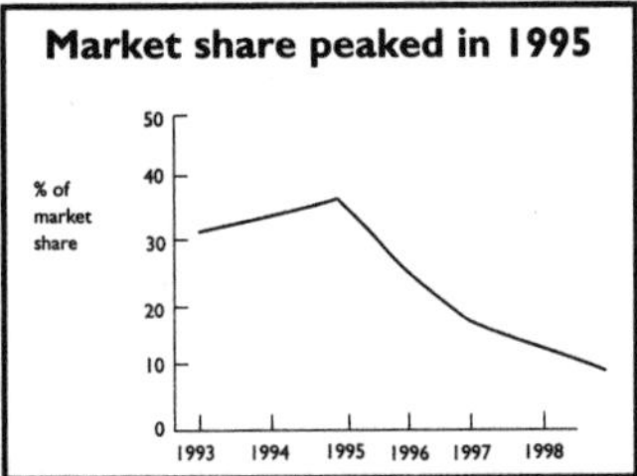

Using "stand-alone sense" Not only should the title make sense on its own, but the wording of the rest of the chart should also make sense to someone seeing it for the first time.

Ineffective: does not make "stand-alone" sense

Hall's Model

High context	**Low context**
• Relationships	• Relationships
• Credibility	• Credibility
• Agreements	• Agreements

Effective: does make "stand-alone" sense

Hall's High Context and Low Context Cultures

High context cultures

- Establish social relationship first.
- Stress personal goodwill credibility.
- Make agreements by general trust.

Low context cultures

- Get down to business first.
- Stress expertise credibility.
- Make agreements by legalistic contracts.

4. Provide transition between each visual.

Finally, when designing tell/sell presentation visuals as a whole, think about how you are going to provide transitions between each visual. Here are three techniques for doing so.

Transition technique #1: Consistency One easy but powerful technique to achieve transitions is to use scrupulous consistency. (1) *Consistency in headings and subheadings:* Each level of headings should adhere to a pattern: use exactly the same font, size, color, and so forth throughout. (2) *Consistency between agenda and "back-ups":* Make sure that the headings in each back-up slide use exactly the same wording as the point in your agenda. For example, if your agenda says "Increase product innovation," the back-up slide should use that exact same wording—not similar wording like "Innovate for new products." (3) *Consistency in numbering system:* If the points are numbered in your agenda, use the same numbering system in your back-up slides.

Transition technique #2: Repeated use of agenda slide Another effective transition tool is to show your agenda slide repeatedly each time you switch to the next main section in your presentation. The following two examples are among the many ways to do so.

Using box to show transition

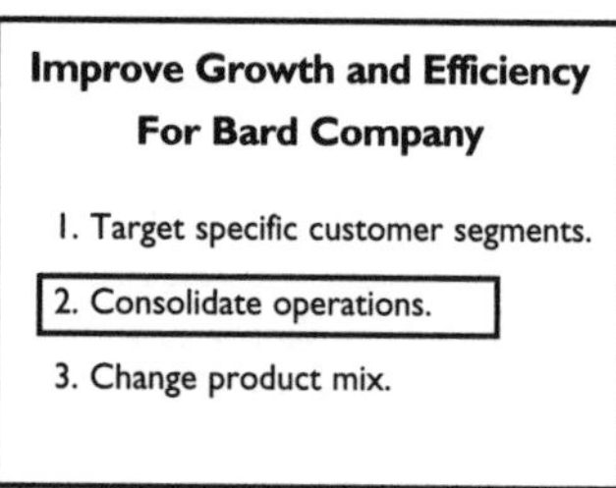

Using "dim" function to show transition

Improve Growth and Efficiency
For Bard Company

1. Target specific customer segments.
2. Consolidate operations.
3. Change product mix.

Transition technique #3: Use of "running headers" If your presentation is especially long or complex, consider using "running headers"—that is, a small restatement of the main section on each slide, similar to the running header at the top of the pages of this and other book chapters. Here are a few of the many ways to use running headers.

Running header: upper left corner

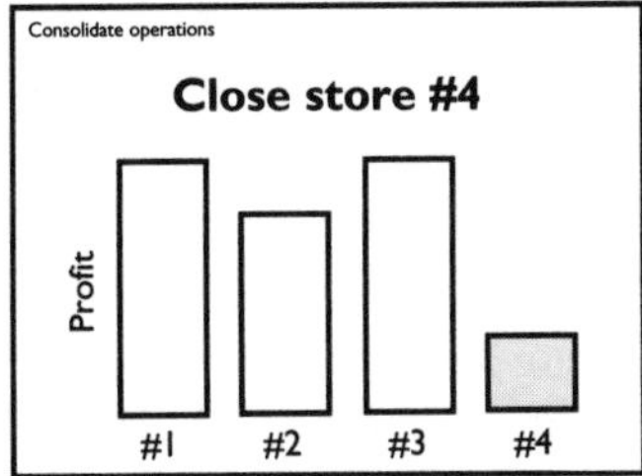

Running header: lower right corner

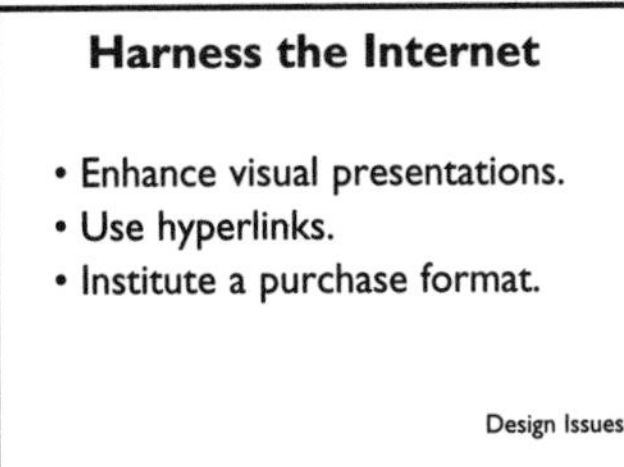

Running header: across top of the page

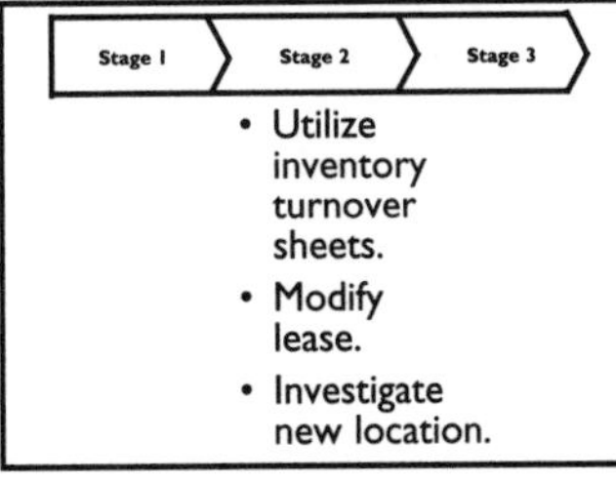

II. DESIGNING EACH INDIVIDUAL CHART

VISUAL AIDS			
I. Designing the presentation as a whole	II. Designing each individual chart	III. Choosing visual aid equipment	IV. Using visual aids effectively

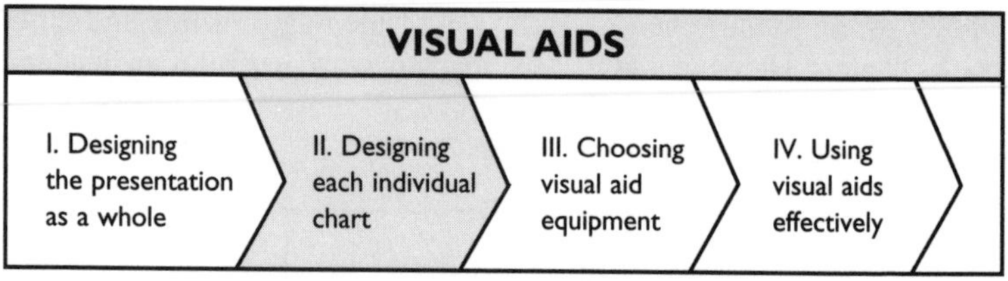

Once you have planned your presentation as a whole, as described in the previous section, then design each individual chart. This section covers design techniques to do so: (1) designing graphs to show quantitative data, (2) designing diagrams to show nonquantitative concepts, (3) designing word charts to show main ideas, (4) using typography effectively, (5) using color effectively, and (6) editing each chart.

1. Designing graphs to show quantitative data

Many business presentations include quantitative data, such as financial information, marketing projections, or operations analyses. In many cases, this kind of data will be easier to comprehend and retain if you show it on graphs—such as line charts or bar charts—rather than just in words and figures—such as lists, tabular charts, spreadsheets, or financial statements. For a tell presentation, in which you simply want to present data without any interpretation, you might choose to show quantitative data non-graphically. However, most business presentations are tell/sell style, in which you want to draw conclusions or even make recommendations for your audience. In these cases, you will be more effective, emphatic, and persuasive if you use graphs. (See pages 6-7 for more on tell versus sell styles.)

Example: data shown non-graphically,
trend not readily apparent

1996		1997	
January	12,543	January	16,985
February	14,371	February	16,106
March	15,998	March	15,422
April	15,004	April	15,010
May	15,281	May	14,564
June	15,742	June	13,820
July	16,101	July	12,489
August	16,254	August	11,376
September	16,378	September	10,897
October	16,495	October	10,178
November	16,397	November	9,657
December	16,463	December	9,281

Same example: data shown graphically,
trend more apparent

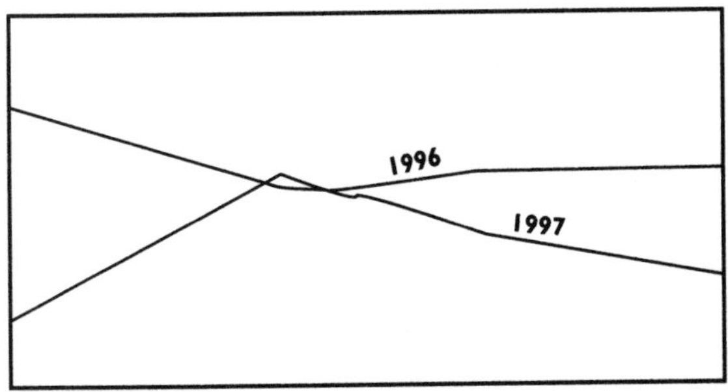

Choose from among the following prevalent chart types to show quantitative data graphically. In addition to those shown, other chart types include grouped line charts (with more than one line), grouped bar charts (with more than one bar for each item), sliding bar charts (with a line down the middle of the page, and bars on the positive and negative sides), and various other combinations.

GRAPHS TO SHOW QUANTITATIVE DATA

If you want to show	Use this graph	Tips
Compenents of one item → • Percentages • Shares • Proportions	**Pie** 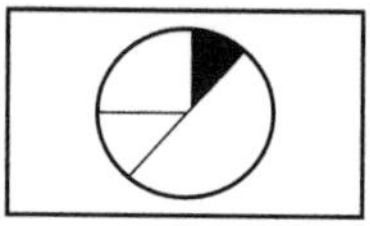 Entire item broken into components	Arrange with most important component at 12 o'clock. If components are equally important, arrange from smallest to largest. Usually, limit to no more than five components.
Rank comparison → • Difference between • Variation • More or less	**Bar** 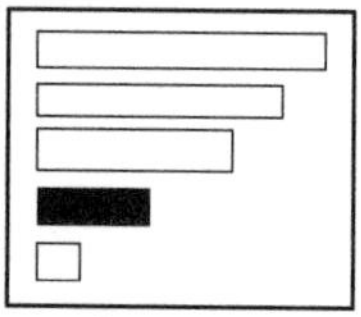 Amount	Arrange in order to suit your needs: alphabetical, low to high, high to low. Bar charts run sideways so they are easier to label. Column charts may imply a time sequence.
Component parts of more than one item → • Percentages • Shares • Proportions	**Subdivided bar or subdivided column** 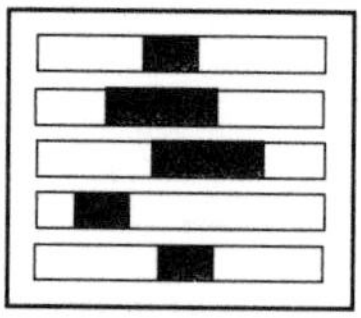 Series of items broken into components	Arrange in order to suit your needs: alphabetical, low to high by a certain component, low to high by item, etc. Bar charts run sideways so they are easier to label. Column charts may imply a time sequence.

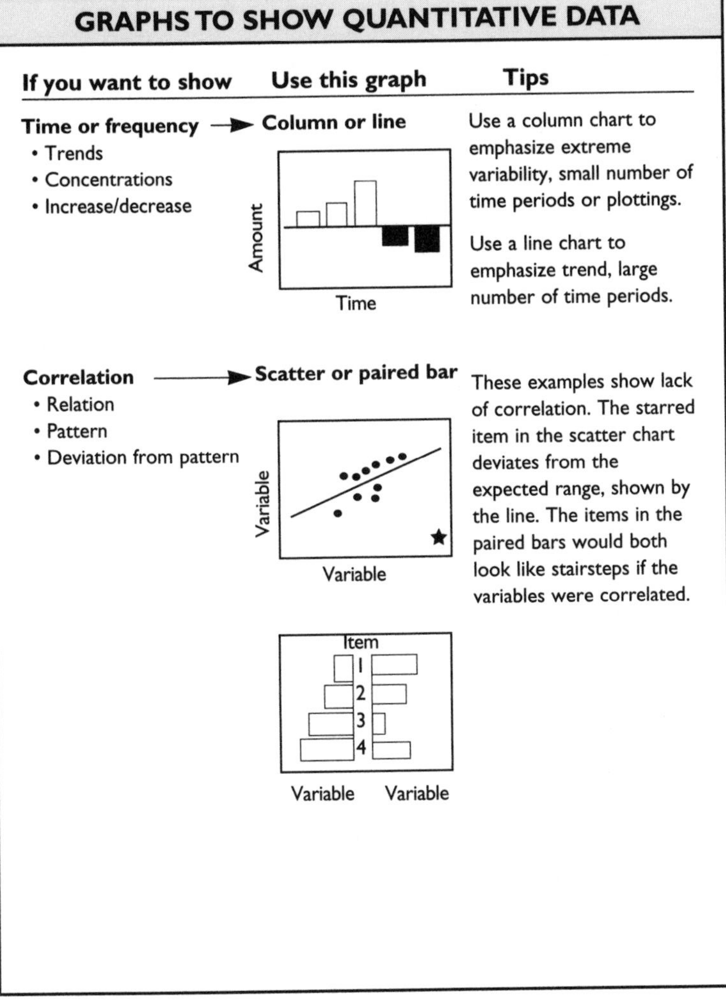

GRAPHS TO SHOW QUANTITATIVE DATA

If you want to show	Use this graph	Tips
Time or frequency → • Trends • Concentrations • Increase/decrease	**Column or line**	Use a column chart to emphasize extreme variability, small number of time periods or plottings. Use a line chart to emphasize trend, large number of time periods.
Correlation → • Relation • Pattern • Deviation from pattern	**Scatter or paired bar**	These examples show lack of correlation. The starred item in the scatter chart deviates from the expected range, shown by the line. The items in the paired bars would both look like stairsteps if the variables were correlated.

LABELING GRAPHS

1. Preferred option: Label inside section

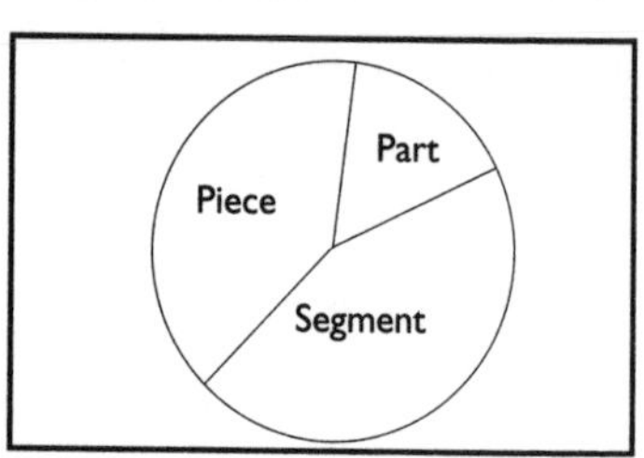

2. Label just outside section

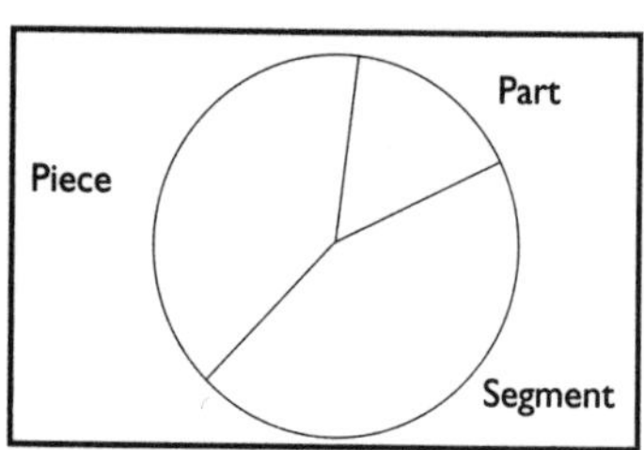

3. Label and connect to section with line

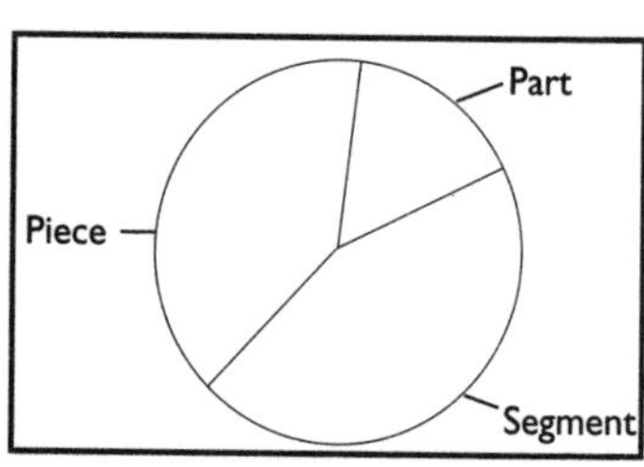

4. Worst option: Use a legend

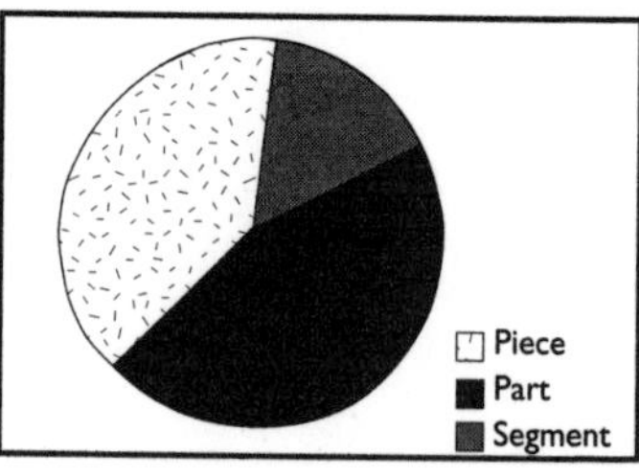

SHOWING EMPHASIS ON GRAPHS

1. Contrasting color

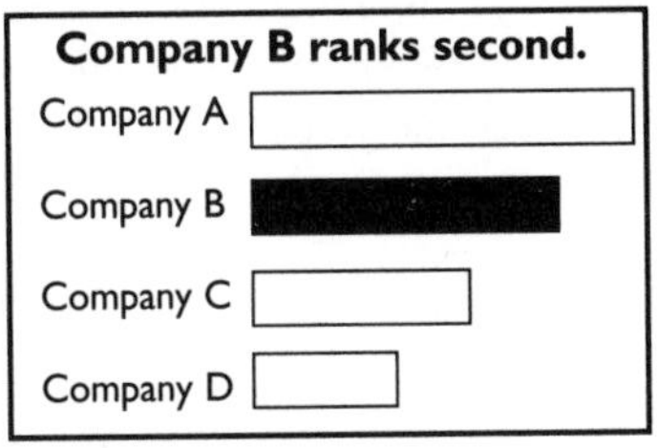

Company B ranks second.

Company A
Company B
Company C
Company D

2. Lines

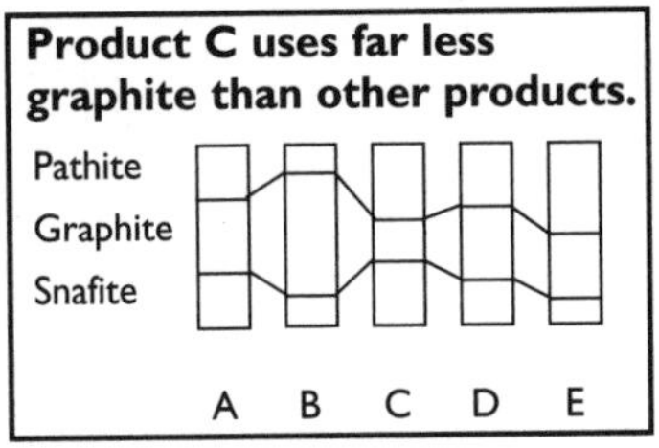

Product C uses far less graphite than other products.

Pathite
Graphite
Snafite
A B C D E

3. Arrows

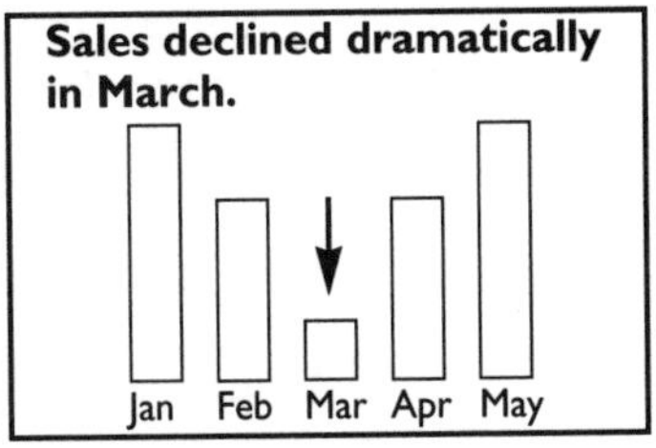

Sales declined dramatically in March.

Jan Feb Mar Apr May

4. "Exploded" off

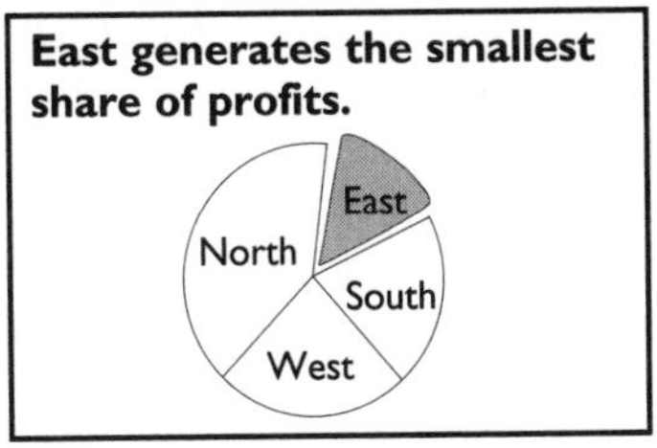

East generates the smallest share of profits.

East
North
South
West

2. Designing diagrams to shown nonquantitative concepts

In addition to showing quantitative data visually on graphs, think about ways in which you can show nonquantitative relationships visually on diagrams, especially to add excitement to your visuals and to reach the 40 percent of your audience who are probably visual learners. For example, compare the two agenda charts below:

Agenda example: words only

Improve Growth and Efficiency for Bard Company

1. Target specific customer segments.
2. Consolidate operations.
3. Change product mix.

Same agenda: showing relationships visually using a diagram

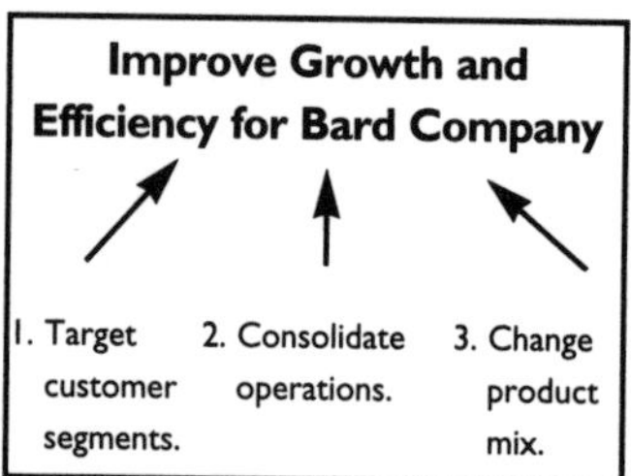

The following examples provide some ideas on how to use diagrams to show nonquantitative data graphically. Other examples of nonquantitative graphs include maps, flowcharts, organization charts, timelines, time-and-activity charts, Gantt charts, and pictograms (e.g., a pound sterling sign representing money). For many more examples of both quantitative and nonquantitative visuals, see Gene Zelazny's fine book, *Say It With Charts,* listed in the bibliography, page 194.

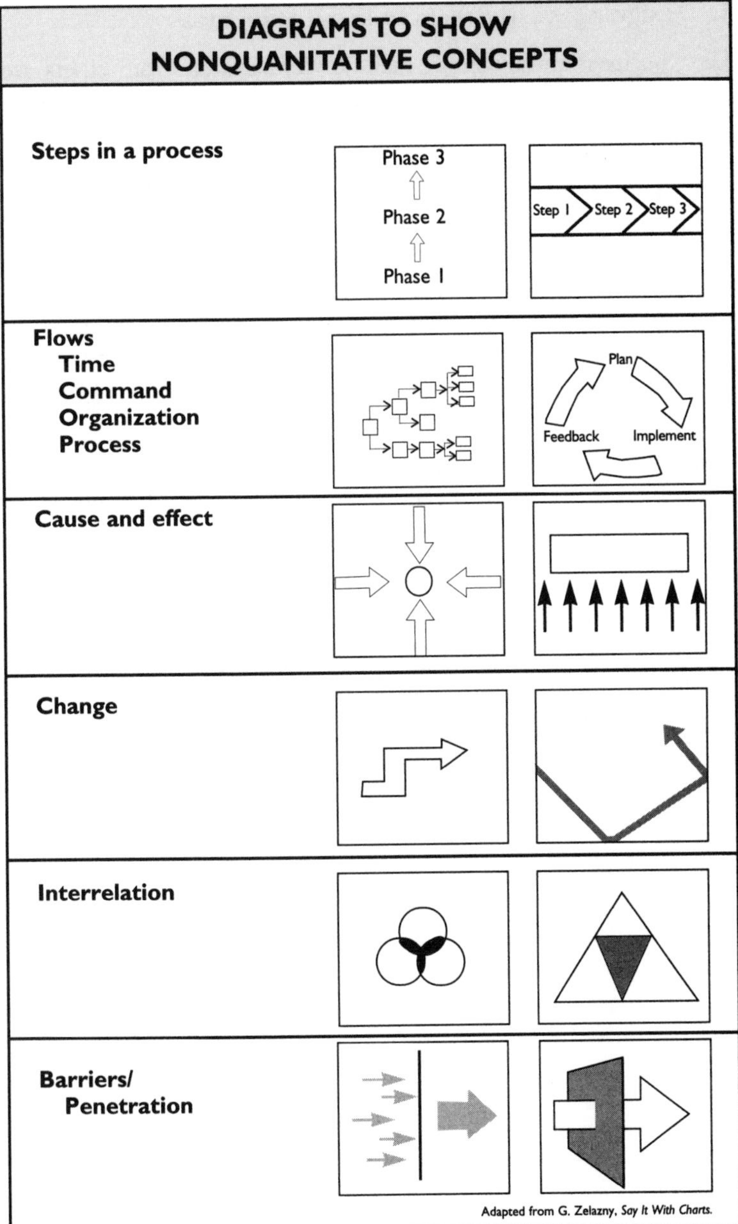
DIAGRAMS TO SHOW
NONQUANITATIVE CONCEPTS
Steps in a process
Phase 3
Phase 2
Phase 1
Step 1
Step 2
Step 3
Flows
Time
Command
Organization
Process
Plan
Feedback
Implement
Cause and effect
Change
Interrelation
Barriers/
Penetration
Adapted from G. Zelazny, *Say It With Charts.*

3. Designing word charts to show main ideas

Most business presentations include word charts. Word charts are effective for reinforcing the main ideas and structure of your presentation. The most pervasive problem with word charts is that they are overused—in part because it is sometimes easier to include everything than to decide what's worth including. If you include every point, then you lose your ability to emphasize certain points. This section shows you how to avoid word charts that are unnecessary and wordy, hard to follow because of lack of parallelism, and hard to read because of ineffective indentation. One final word of wisdom: do not undercut your credibility with spelling errors on your word charts. Spelling errors are often more noticeable and glaring on a large screen in front of a group than they are in a document.

Avoid wordiness. Avoid overusing word charts, especially boring word-for-word scripts that echo what you are saying throughout the entire presentation. Pare down your word charts to include key words and phrases only.

Ineffective chart: too wordy

Introduction

Over the past two decades, the waste management industry has undertaken planning as a response to growing markets and an increasingly competitive environment. Understanding historical environmental trends and how they are expected to change is critical to the development of successful strategies for Boford Industries.

The purpose of this presentation is to:

- Examine the waste management industry today and how it got there
- Assess future trends and their implications
- Discuss how other companies are reacting and changing in response to the external environment

Effective chart: key phrases only

Presentation Agenda
Boford Industries

- Examine historical trends
- Assess future trends
- Analyze competition

Use grammatical parallelism. Use grammatical parallelism on word charts—that is, make sure the first word in a series is consistent with the other first words in that series. Like spelling errors, parallelism problems are often more noticeable on visuals than they are on documents because they are projected on a large screen.

Ineffective: not grammatically parallel

Steps to organize internally

1. Establishing formal sales organization
2. Production department responsibilities defined
3. Improve cost-accounting system

Effective: grammatically parallel

Steps to organize internally

1. Establish formal sales organization.
2. Define responsibilities for the production department.
3. Improve cost-accounting system.

Use conceptual parallelism. Word charts need to be not only grammatically parallel, but also conceptually parallel—that is, ideas of equal importance should be shown at equal hierarchical levels.

Ineffective: not conceptually parallel:
all three lines are not of equal importance

- Change product mix.
- Eliminate Product X.
- Concentrate on Product Y.

Effective: conceptually parallel:
first line is more general;
second and third lines are of equal importance

Change product mix.

- Eliminate Product X.
- Concentrate on Product Y.

Use effective indentation. Finally, word charts are easier to read if entire sections are indented, as shown below.

Ineffective indentation

1. Here is an example of a numbered section in which the number does not stand out very much because the subsequent lines "wrap around" the number.

 1. Here is another example of a numbered section in which the number does not stand out very much, this time because only the first line is indented.

Effective indentation

1. Here is an example of an effective numbered indentation; all lines in the section are indented equally, so the number "stands out" on its own.

4. Using typography effectively

Typography—including font, size, use of boldface, italics, capitals, and so forth—is an important feature of both graphic and word charts. One of the most prevalent problems with visuals is literally unreadable lettering. Choose your typography with care: large enough, readable, and clear.

Using large enough letters Make sure that each letter is large enough for everyone in your audience to see. The only sure test is to sit in the seat farthest from the visuals and see if you can read the lettering. If you are using computer-generated visuals, normally you should use at least 18-point type, and more often 24- or 36-point type.

Readable size

This is 24-point type.

Less readable size

This is 12-point type. It is fine for written documents, but too small for overhead transparencies.

Using standard capitalization Except for very short titles, capitalize only the first letter of a sentence or phrase.

Readable capitalization

This is standard capitalization. Only the first letter of the phrase or sentence is capitalized.

Less readable capitalization

This Is Not Standard Capitalization. Capitalizing Every Word Slows Down Your Reader.

Least readable capitalization

THIS IS ALL CAPITALS. THE LACK OF SIZE VARIATION WITH ALL CAPITAL LETTERS MAKES THIS KIND OF TEXT HARD TO READ.

Choosing a readable font As explained on pages 57-58, serif fonts are the easiest to read. *Serif fonts* are those with extenders on the ends of most letters; *sans serif fonts* do not have extenders on the ends of letters. A sans serif font with all capital letters is the hardest to read, as shown in the following example.

Ineffective typography: sans serif, all capitals

THIS IS A SANS SERIF FONT, SET IN ALL CAPITAL LETTERS. THE LACK OF SIZE VARIATION WITH ALL CAPITALS AND NO SERIFS MAKES THIS COMBINATION THE HARDEST TO READ.

Avoiding "letterjunk" *Letterjunk* is the gratuitous use of lettering that calls undue attention to itself or is simply hard to read. Examples of letterjunk include too many typographical elements (such as, boldface plus italics plus underlining plus all capitals all at once), outline and shadow styles, arty fonts, and jarring font variations.

Ineffective typography: examples of "letterjunk"

THIS SHOWS BOLDFACE + UNDERLINING + ALL CAPS!

This shows shadow style.

This shows an "arty" font.

This shows jarring font variations.

5. Using color effectively

Use of color can make your visuals look attractive, lively, professional, and memorable; emphasize important ideas; and show your structure. On the other hand, for some audiences, use of color can come across as too slick or too expensive (even if, in fact, using color is not that expensive) and can run counter to cultural norms or expectations. If using color is appropriate, here are some suggestions for doing so. Although the examples below emphasize slides, remember that a little bit of color will also go a long way to improve your flipchart design.

What to color Use color to serve a function, not merely to decorate.

- *To reinforce the logic of your structure:* Viewers sense color relationships clearly, so they will stay better attuned to your structure if you use color. Throughout the entire presentation, use exactly the same pattern (including not only color, but also size and font) for your main headings, secondary headings, running headings, and so forth.
- *For emphasis:* Viewers look at anything that is not black and white first, so another effective use of color is for emphasis or to show priority. For example, if you want to emphasize one "slice of the pie" in a pie chart, use a bright, contrasting color for that slice only. Many computer graphic programs automatically color every pie slice or bar or column a different color, which tends to overwhelm the audience with too much visual stimulation. Override these programs to control what you want to emphasize; use no more than two colors plus black and white. Tie the colored element to your message title, as explained on page 114. Do not use color for unemphatic elements only, e. g., bullet points or lines only. (See page 123 for other emphasis techniques.)

What colors to choose Keep in mind the following intrinsic characteristics of some colors.

- *Receding and advancing colors:* Some colors command more attention than others. The cool colors (blue, green, and violet) are "receding" colors, so they make good background colors. Warm colors (red, orange and yellow) are "advancing" colors; they will attract more attention. Yellow has maximum visibility. Overuse of warm colors can actually increase anxiety and raise your audience's blood pressure.

- *Cultural connotations of color:* In the Anglo-American culture, the cool colors connote calmness and authority; the warm colors connote dynamism and activity; the dark colors (black, gray, dark gray) evoke power and strength. Use of red with monetary totals can imply "in the red." However, these emotional overtones vary by individual and by culture. For example, although black connotes death in Western cultures, the death color is white in many Eastern cultures, yellow in many Moslem cultures, and purple in many Latin American cultures. As another example, the colors of a country's flag will have a special meaning in that country. Finally, use colors that are consistent with your organization's corporate identity.
- *Color-blindness:* Remember that eight percent of men and one percent of women are color-blind, so avoid using green and red as contrasting colors. Blue is a universally recognized color.

Selecting a color template If you are using computer software for your visuals, select a color template—a combination of background and foreground colors—to use consistently throughout the presentation for a unified look. Most of the standardized templates available on computer software packages are inappropriate for most business presentations; they tend to be fanciful and cutesy and to draw too much attention to themselves. Create your own template to be more appropriate for your particular audience.

- *Background color:* Select your background color based on the equipment you will be using: for a well-lit room (for example, for some overhead projectors), choose a light background, such as pale blue or white; for a darkened room (for example, for some multimedia projectors), choose a dark background, such as dark blue or black.
- *Foreground color:* Your foreground color—that is, for titles and text—should contrast sharply with the background color (e.g., yellow or white on navy or dark blue, but not yellow on white or light blue on dark blue).
- *Repeated elements:* Choose relatively unobtrusive colors for elements repeated on each visual—such as borders, lines, or logos.

6. Editing each chart

Just as you micro edit your writing (pages 67-83), you also micro edit your visuals. In addition to cutting wordiness, as discussed on page 126, edit overload and extraneous graphics.

Avoid overload. Avoid overloaded text or graphic visuals that include too much complexity for one chart. Audience members may end up reading and pondering these charts instead of listening to you; at worst, they may get completely lost. Therefore, for each visual, decide what is most important for the audience to see. If you find yourself with an overloaded visual, such as the one shown below, you might choose: (1) to simplify it so that the key ideas, figures, or trends are emphasized, as illustrated below, or (2) to cut it so that one section is shown in detail, as illustrated below, or (3) to break it into a series of overlays or progressive "builds," each showing added layers of detail.

Ineffective chart: overloaded

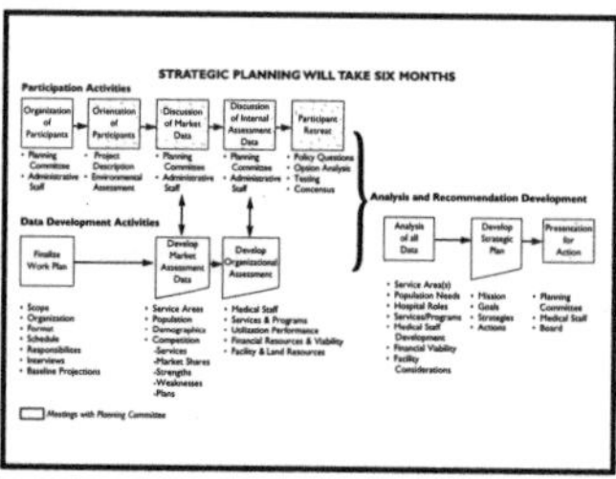

Effective chart: simplified to show key trends only

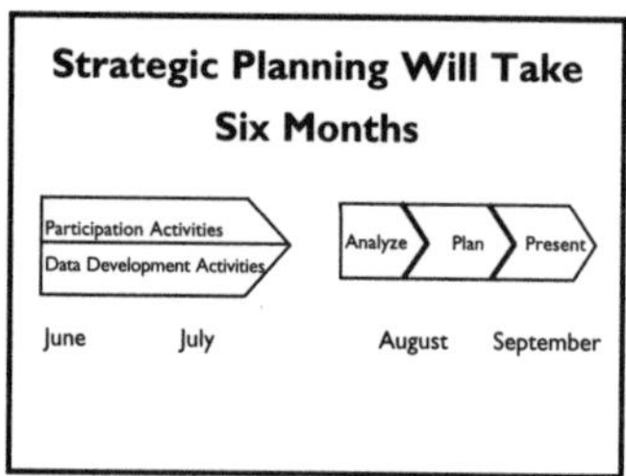

Delete extraneous graphics. To use the term coined by visual aids expert Edward Tufte, delete "chartjunk"—any design elements that do not contribute to your message:

- *Decorations* that do not add informational value—such as unnecessary shading, unnecessary borders, misleading three-dimensional effects, unnecessary decorations, and "op art" cross-hatching.
- *Legends* and confusing cross-coding systems that take longer for your audience to comprehend than labeling the parts of the pie charts, bar charts, line charts, and so forth right on the pie, bar, or lines themselves.

Ineffective chart: "chartjunk"

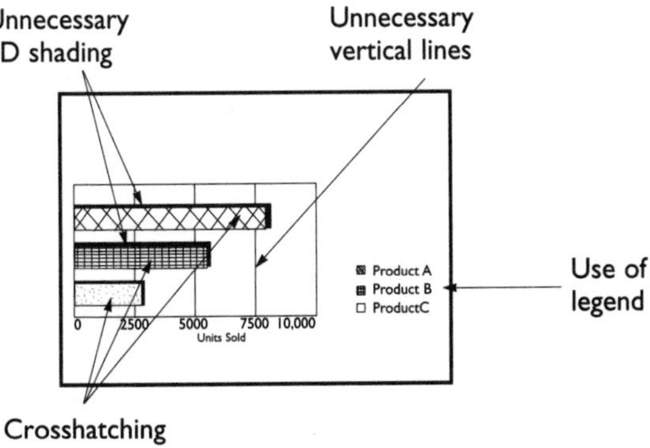

Effective chart: no "chartjunk"

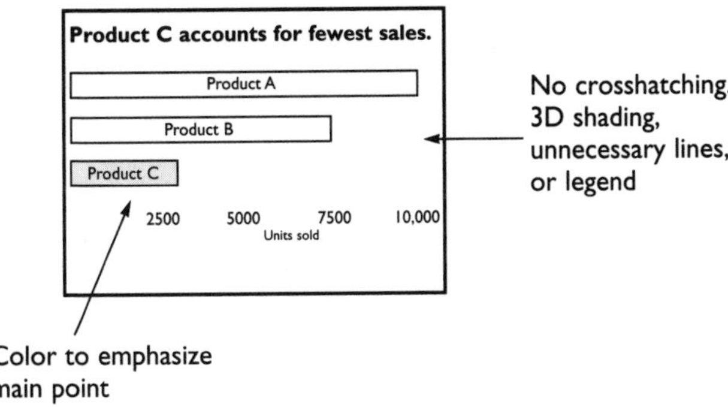

III. CHOOSING VISUAL AID EQUIPMENT

VISUAL AIDS			
I. Designing the presentation as a whole	II. Designing each individual chart	III. Choosing visual aid equipment	IV. Using visual aids effectively

To choose your visual aids equipment, first consider three sets of issues:

- *Expectations:* What are the expectations of your particular audience, organization, and culture regarding equipment?
- *Audience size:* Consider also the number of people in your audience. For example, for a group of three or four, a packet of handouts might be a better choice than a multimedia presentation. For a group of ten, a flipchart might work well; it would be unreadable for a group of 80.
- *Availability:* Finally, be realistic about the equipment and resources you have available.

Only after you have answered these three questions, think about the intrinsic characteristics of the various kinds of equipment—which are described below, with advantages and disadvantages listed on the chart on pages 136-137.

Multimedia projection systems Multimedia systems project images and sounds from a personal computer, the World Wide Web, videotape, or audiotape. If you are putting data into a computer during a multimedia presentation, you may want to ask someone else to input the information while you talk. Three kinds of multimedia projectors are:

- *Large-screen projectors:* Large-screen projectors, also known as data/video projectors, have the best color quality and picture resolution of the multimedia systems.
- *LCD projection panels:* These panels connect to the video output of a PC, but they are placed on top of, or built into, an overhead projector's glass. They are effective for small groups on a small screen.
- *Portable computers:* A computer is an effective option with a group that is small enough so all can see the PC screen. They have higher resolution and consistency than the other two multimedia systems.

Still projection systems Three varieties of still projectors are overhead projectors, 35 mm slide projectors, and CCD digital cameras.

- *Overhead projectors:* Overhead projectors are extremely versatile: you can write on them real time, you can prepare them entirely in advance, and you can easily refer back to a slide or change the order.
- *35 mm slide projectors:* Thirty-five millimeter slides have the highest resolution and truest color of all the still projection systems. However, you have to fast-forward to get to the slide you want to show.
- *CCD digital cameras:* CCD digital cameras—also known as document cameras or copy stands—create a digital image and magnify it onto a screen. These are often used to magnify and digitalize documents or objects during a videoconference.

Animated projection systems Animated projection systems—including video and film—are good for large audiences. However, they require a darkened room.

Boards and charts Boards and charts often elicit the best group discussions.

- *Traditional black or white boards:* These may encourage group discussion because they are low tech and unintimidating; however, they do not provide hard copy.
- *Electronic copy boards:* These provide hard copy of anything you place or write on the board. The presenter can annotate these real time with an infrared pen.
- *"Live" boards:* These can be annotated real-time in multiple locations, and some have application-sharing capabilities.
- *Flipcharts:* Flipcharts may be prepared in advance or written as you speak; they include desktop charts and standing flipcharts.

Handouts Handouts provide hard copy for your audience to take away with them, but the audience can read ahead and become distracted from what you are saying. Therefore, give only those handouts you don't mind people reading at the beginning of your presentation; give handouts with detailed information at the moment you are discussing it; and save detailed summary handouts until the end of the presentation. The advantage of electronic handouts is that instead of having to carry papers, the audience can access material when they want to from the network or disk.

VISUAL AID EQUIPMENT		
Equipment	**Main advantages**	**Main disadvantages**
	For all multimedia projections	
Multimedia projection systems	Can use input from PC, World Wide Web, video, etc.; can use animation (e.g., show "swoop," etc.); can use a variety of "build" techniques; can plug into audience's networked computers; can input numbers real-time	May be complicated to use; usually need darkened room; not good for facilitating group discussion; cannot annotate real-time; may appear too slick for some audiences
	All of the above plus	***All of the above plus***
Large-screen projectors	Best color quality and picture resolution; good if need 5′ x 7′ screen; projector does not block audience view	May have portability or compatibility problems in different locations
LDC projection panels	Portability; good for smaller groups, smaller screen	Less effective resolution on large screen
Portable computers	Portability; good for very small groups who can all see PC screen	Cannot use with large group
	For all still projection systems	
Still projection systems	Portability; less technically complex than multimedia; compatibility problems unlikely; easy to use	No animation
	All of the above plus	***All of the above plus***
Overhead projectors	Versatile: can write on them real-time or prepare completely in advance; "random access": easy to refer back to a previous slide; can make image large or small	Somewhat darkened room; projector may block audience view; may be awkward to manipulate; may appear old-fashioned to some audiences
35 mm slide projectors	Highest resolution, truest color, of all projection systems; projection does not block audience view visible to large audiences, e.g., in an auditorium	Darkened room; may be time-consuming to produce 35 mm slides; "serial access": hard to refer back to a previous slide easily; cannot annotate real-time

CCD digital cameras	Projects image from any hard copy or 3D object	
	For all animated projection systems	
Animated projection systems	Animated; visible to large audiences, e.g., in an auditorium	Darkened room; "serial access:" hard to refer back to specific section easily
	All of the above plus	***All of the above plus***
Video projections	Interruptions possible using start, stop, rewind, pause; audiences with networked PC's can access video directly	Format must be compatibile in different locations, especially in different countries (PALS vs. VHS)
	For all boards and charts	
Boards and charts	Brightly-lit room; good for facilitating group discussion; can annotate real-time	Inability to show complex images; usually too small to be seen by a large group
	All of the above plus	***All of the above plus***
Traditional black or white boards	May encourage discussion because low-tech, unintimidating	Must erase to regain free space; no hard copy; may appear unprofessional
Electronic copy boards	Provides digitalized hard copy of document computer files or 2D object; can be annotated real-time in one location; can be viewed on computer screen at multiple locations	Must erase to regain free space; same limitations as a scanner, free-format
Live boards	All of the above, plus (1) can be annotated on-line in multiple locations; (2) may have application-sharing capability	
Flipcharts	No electronics problems; may be prepared in advance or annotated real-time	Large and clumsy to transport
	For all handouts	
	Provides hard copy; shows complex data; can be used for audience note-taking	Audience can read ahead and become distracted from what you are saying

IV. USING VISUAL AIDS EFFECTIVELY

VISUAL AIDS			
I. Designing the presentation as a whole	II. Designing each individual chart	III. Choosing visual aid equipment	IV. Using visual aids effectively

All your work composing and designing visual aids will be wasted unless you use them effectively during the presentation itself. This section covers techniques for using visuals effectively: (1) using visuals prepared in advance (in tell/sell presentations) and (2) facilitating group discussions with visuals (in consult/join situations).

1. Using visuals prepared in advance.

Here are seven suggestions for using prepared visuals gracefully, unobtrusively, and effectively.

Become familiar with your equipment. Get extremely comfortable with your equipment before the presentation. This suggestion sounds obvious, yet many speakers have had their entire credibility and confidence undercut because the projector wouldn't function properly or the charts were upside down. Practice with your equipment: actually turn on the projector, press the buttons, use the mouse or remote control, flip the pages. Make sure you know how to insert the cassette, position the slides, write large enough, and so forth. Practice with any given piece of equipment long enough so you can use it casually.

Show only the chart you are discussing. Make sure your audience will see the same information you are talking about.

- *Opening:* For your presentation opening, figure out a way to cover any visuals you don't want people to see yet. For example, use a "title page," a blank screen or page, or leave the projector turned off until you get to your first chart.

- *After each visual:* When you are no longer discussing a visual, get it out of sight. For example, insert a blank slide if you aren't using another visual for several minutes; erase the board; or detach and post, the page you're finished with, or turn to a blank page, for a flipchart.

Introduce each visual. Remember that, although you may be intimately familiar with the visual, this is the first time the audience will see it. Give them a chance to become acquainted with the chart before you start to talk in detail about one part of it. For a simple text visual, you might say: "As this agenda chart shows, I will cover three main topics today" (then list and point to each of the three). For a complicated graphic visual, explain the graph in general first; you might say, "As you can see, this graph covers each month of the last fiscal year on the horizontal axis (point to it) and sales in thousands of dollars on the vertical axis (point to it). In particular, I'd like to draw your attention to the May figures (point to them)." If the chart is particularly complex, introduce the chart section-by-section with a series of "builds" or overlays, instead of putting it up in its entirety all at once.

Meter out information on each chart. Your audience will always read whatever is in front of them, regardless of what you are saying; they can read faster than you can talk. Therefore, use a metering technique of your choice to control exactly when your audience sees each line.

- *Multimedia projectors:* With multimedia projectors, you can use the "build" function to add new lines of information. (See page 116 for an example.)
- *Overhead projectors:* With overhead projectors, you can (1) use a series of overlays, (2) write preplanned information as you discuss it, or (3) use a "mask" or piece of cardboard to cover up information until you want it to show—although some audience members may resent this technique.

Use handouts effectively. With handouts, be particularly cautious; people will always read ahead. Think about when to distribute them.

- *At the beginning:* Give some handouts at the beginning of your presentation: general handouts, such as agendas; handouts you don't mind people reading ahead; or handouts with blank space for audience note-taking.

- *Not until you discuss:* Distribute handouts with detailed information (too complex for a chart) only at the specific point in your presentation when you are discussing it. Remember to give the audience some time to read what they were just handed.
- *At the end:* Detailed summary handouts you don't want your audience to read ahead, and handouts downloaded from the screen, distribute at the end of the presentation.

Use pointing effectively. Pointing is an extremely effective technique. It enhances your nonverbal delivery by giving you something to do with your hands, and it enhances audience comprehension by reinforcing what you're saying with what they're seeing. Here are some tips for effective pointing:

- *Point to the exact place:* Point at the exact place on your chart you want the audience to look; do not merely gesture vaguely in the direction of your visual.
- *Face your audience:* Regardless of whether you are right- or left-handed, always point with whichever hand is closest to the screen or chart, so you will not put your back to the audience.
- *Point on the screen itself:* If possible, point on the screen itself, not on the overhead projector; projectors magnify any nervousness you might be showing in your hands or fingers.
- *Point with your hand:* If possible, point with your hand—not with any kind of pointer—unless you absolutely cannot reach what you are pointing to otherwise. Pointers usually cause fidgeting and shaking problems; if you must use a pointer, practice with it extensively to avoid these problems.

Look at your audience. Many speakers get so engrossed with their equipment or charts that they forget to look at the audience. Remember, you are there to interact with your audience, not with your visuals. Practice maintaining your eye contact while using visuals.

- *Using projectors:* If you are using any kind of projector, face your audience—not the screen, the projector, or the computer. If possible, stand next to the screen. If you stand next to the projector or the computer itself, you may block some people's view of the screen.
- *Writing:* If you are writing as you speak, avoid writing for long periods of time. Write key phrases only; use abbreviations. You also might trace over figures you have drawn very faintly in advance to avoid having your back to the audience for too long.

2. Facilitating group discussions with visuals

On pages 96-105, we discussed consult/join situations—such as meetings or brainstorming sessions. In these situations, you will not present prepared visual aids as you would in a tell/sell presentation. Instead, you will use visuals to enhance interaction: to record participant comments, to summarize action plans, and to form the basis for meeting minutes. The following section explains how to use visuals to facilitate group discussions.

Why use visuals to facilitate discussion In a group collaboration or meeting, you should almost always record ideas on some kind of visual, such as a board or chart. Why?

- *For accuracy:* Recording ideas publicly ensures accuracy and a record of what was said.
- *For morale:* Recording ideas publicly also makes people feel heard and appreciated, even if their ideas are rejected later.
- *For timing control:* Besides making everyone feel included and heard, writing on visuals may be used to control timing. If people talk too long or repetitively, recording their points may assure them of feeling heard, so you can move on.
- *For a permanent record:* From your charts, you can come up with a permanent record at the end of the meeting, either electronically if you have an electronic board or by writing minutes from the charts. (See page 103 for suggestions on meeting follow-up.)

How to plan visuals for group discussions Although most of the work involved with recording a discussion goes on during the session itself, be sure to plan your charts and logistics in advance.

- *Tie them to the agenda:* Your visuals should follow from your agenda; they should be organized precisely as your agenda states.
- *Decide on headings:* Your headings in consult/join visuals are just as important as they are in tell/sell visuals. Since you want your audience to offer ideas, each heading should remind them what they are discussing. Therefore, decide in advance what your main headings are going to be. In most cases, write the main headings up in advance, leaving space to fill in as ideas are generated. For example, list various options across the board or provide a heading at the top of a chart describing what you are brainstorming about.

- *Consider logistics:* Think about the logistics of the room—such as where to put empty charts and where to post filled-in charts.

How to choose equipment Think about your equipment choice in advance. Regardless of what equipment you choose, make sure it works; in particular, check to make sure all the markers work. See pages 134-137 for more detail on equipment.

- *Flipcharts:* One popular equipment choice for group discussions is flipcharts. Flipcharts can be taped up around the room for reference during the session, and you can take them with you for a permanent record at the end of the session.
- *Electronic boards:* Another good choice is electronic boards or "live boards," which provide a hard copy of what was written on them—unlike traditional boards, which need to be erased when they are full.
- *Overheads:* Finally, although it is technically possible to use overheads to record people's ideas, remember that some people associate overheads with a tell/sell presentation rather than with a discussion, and may be less likely to talk.

Why to consider using a scribe Instead of writing on the visuals yourself, consider asking someone else to serve as scribe. However, determining what to record and when to record it is a tool of control and influence, so if you use someone else as scribe, make it extremely clear in advance how you will work together: you may, for example, want to specify that the scribe records only the specific wording you signal to him or her to write down during the session; or you may trust the scribe to record at his or her discretion. This increasingly popular technique offers three benefits:

- *Enhances facilitation:* Managing the discussion will be much easier for you, because you don't have to talk and write at the same time.
- *Improves legibility:* The scribe can write more carefully and you can select someone with neat handwriting.
- *Saves time:* Perhaps most important, using a scribe saves time, because you can go on to discuss the next point while the scribe is still recording the previous point.

How to record on visuals Writing to record participants' ideas is not easy. Here are six suggestions to improve your effectiveness:

- *Record accurately:* If you are facilitating the meeting or brainstorming session, paraphrase the comment verbally, and, if the speaker seems satisfied, record it on the chart. If you are not facilitating, but just serving as scribe, either record the facilitator's paraphrase, or if the facilitator has not paraphrased verbally, check with the speaker verbally ("OK?" or "Is this what you mean?") or nonverbally (questioning eye contact), to make sure what you've written is accurate.
- *Record essential phrases only:* Make sure you record essential words and phrases only. Don't bore your audience by laboriously writing long, complex sentences.
- *Include all comments:* Write down everybody's comments—not just some people's. You don't want to appear to be ignoring people or leaving people out. Recording their ideas on your visuals does not necessarily mean you agree with them; instead, it means you hear and acknowledge them. In fact, you may very well end up recording contradictory ideas. That is perfectly appropriate in an interactive session; you can go back later and evaluate the comments. (See pages 99-101.)
- *Keep charts in full view:* Be sure to write in full view of the group and post all charts in full view of the group throughout the meeting, so everyone can see what's going on.
- *Use large enough lettering:* Make sure your writing is large enough. Before the session, seat yourself in the last row to check your lettering size. You may be surprised how large you need to write.
- *Write neatly:* You can learn to write more neatly with practice—or, if you simply have messy writing, consider using a scribe to record for you.

See the checklists on pages 162-163 for a summary of all the speaking issues covered in Chapters V, VI, and VII: structure, visual aids, and nonverbal delivery.

CHAPTER VII OUTLINE

I. Nonverbal "sending": delivery skills
   1. Body language
   2. Vocal qualities
   3. Space and objects
   4. Practice and arrangements
   5. Physical relaxation
   6. Mental relaxation
   7. Last-minute relaxation

II. Nonverbal "receiving": listening skills
   1. Attending skills
   2. Encouraging skills
   3. Following skills

CHAPTER VII

Speaking: Nonverbal Skills

Your words (Chapter V) and your visual aids (Chapter VI) make up only a portion of what your communicate. In fact, experts estimate that 65 to 90 percent of what you communicate is nonverbal. This chapter covers those nonverbal messages you send—the way you appear and sound to others.

The first half of the chapter covers nonverbal "sending" skills, called delivery skills. The second half concentrates on nonverbal "receiving" skills, called listening skills. The examples in this chapter are based on Anglo-American business practices; keep in mind that nonverbal communication varies widely across different cultures, as discussed on pages 29-31.

NONVERBAL SKILLS		
Section in this chapter:	**I. Nonverbal "Sending": Delivery Skills**	**II. Nonverbal "Receiving": Listening Skills**
Who speaks most:	You	Your audience
Purposes:	To inform To persuade	To understand
Typical situations:	Tell/sell presentations	Questions and answers Consult/join meetings One-to-one conversations

I. NONVERBAL "SENDING": DELIVERY SKILLS

NONVERBAL SKILLS		
Section in this chapter:	**I. Nonverbal "Sending": Delivery Skills**	**II. Nonverbal "Receiving": Listening Skills**
Who speaks most:	You	Your audience
Purposes:	To inform To persuade	To understand
Typical situations:	Tell/sell presentations	Questions and answers Consult/join meetings One-to-one conversations

Nonverbal delivery skills include: body language, vocal qualities, and space and objects around you.

1. Body language

Keep in mind these five elements of body language.

Posture Effective speakers exhibit poise through their posture.

- Stand in a relaxed, professional manner—comfortably upright, squarely facing your audience, with your weight balanced and distributed evenly. Your feet should be aligned under your shoulders—neither too close nor too far apart.
- Watch out for rocking or swaying side to side, back and forth, or up and down on your toes. Beware also of slouching or keeping your weight on one side or on the podium. Finally, avoid "frozen" poses, such as the stiff "Attention!" stance.

Body movement Body movement varies by personality and room size.

- Move naturally. You don't have to stand stock still or to plan every move. Examples of effective body movement include leaning forward to emphasize a point, or walking back to point to your visual aid.
- Avoid random, nervous, quick, or constant movements.

Hand and arm gestures Effective speakers use their hands the same way they would conversationally: some are expansive, others reserved.

- Let your hands do whatever they would be doing if you were speaking to one person instead of to a group. For example, they might be moving conversationally; they might be still for a while; they might be pointing to an item on your visual aid.
- Avoid putting your hands in any one position and leaving them there without change—such as the "figleaf" (hands clasped in front), the "parade rest" (hands clasped in back), the "gunshot wound" (hand clutching opposite arm), or the "podium clutch." Also avoid nervous-looking gestures, such as ear-tugging or arm-scratching.

Facial expression Your facial expression should also look natural, as it might in conversation.

- Keep your face relaxed, to look interested and animated. Vary your expression, according to the subject and the occasion.
- Avoid a stony, deadpan expression and avoid inappropriate expressions, such as smiling when you are talking about something sad or negative.

Eye contact Eye contact is a crucial nonverbal skill. It exemplifies what communication expert Lynn Russell calls the "listening/speaking connection": with good eye contact, (1) the audience feels connected with you and (2) you can read the audience's reactions.

- Look throughout the entire room, establishing momentary (that is, about two-second) contact with individuals in your audience. You might try, for starters, looking at the friendly faces; their nodding and smiling will encourage you. Eventually, however, you should look at everyone—especially the key decision-makers in the group. You don't need to keep 100 percent eye contact; you may need to look away briefly to think. If, after your presentation, you can remember what the people in your audience looked like, you had good eye contact.
- Avoid looking constantly at a manuscript or note cards, at the visual aids or screen, at the middle of the back of the room, at the ceiling, or at the floor. Don't show a preference for looking at one side of the room or the other. Finally, avoid fake eye contact—such as "eye dart," eyes moving back and forth very rapidly, or the "lighthouse scan."

2. Vocal qualities

Many people underestimate the importance of the voice in establishing credibility. Effective use of the voice involves four components.

Inflection The term *inflection* refers to variations in your volume that create expressive, non-monotone sound.

- Speak with expressiveness and enthusiasm, in a warm, pleasant tone, with a variety of highs and lows in your voice. Use volume appropriate for the size of the room. Breathe deeply and fully.
- Avoid speaking in a boring monotone or in a distracting pitch (such as too high). Do not speak too quietly to be heard or too loudly for the size of the room. Watch out for two particular volume problems: volume drops at the ends of your sentences and volume drops when you use visual aids.

Rate Rate is the speed at which you speak.

- Vary your rate somewhat, to avoid droning. Generally, keep it slow enough to be understood but fast enough to maintain energy. Use pauses before or after a key term, to separate items in a series, or to indicate a major break in thought.
- Watch for the common problem of speaking at a monotonous, constant rate. An ineffective rate lacks pauses or variation: if too slow, it may bore your audience; if too fast, it may lose them.

Fillers Fillers are verbal pauses—like *uh, er, um,* and *ya know.*

- Pause during your presentation to collect your thoughts. You don't need to fill the pause with a filler.
- Don't overreact if you notice a few fillers; everybody uses them occasionally. If you diagnose a distracting, habitual, overuse of fillers, try working to eliminate them in your everyday conversations.

Enunciation Enunciation is the clarity of your pronunciation.

- Pronounce your words clearly, without mumbling, running words together, leaving out syllables, or dropping final consonants.
- Avoid mumbling, which may be perceived as sounding uneducated or hurried. Avoid running words together—as in *gonna* or *wanna*—which is often associated with talking too fast. Avoid leaving out syllables, as in *guvmint*. Finally, avoid dropping final consonants, as in *thousan', jus',* or *goin'*.

3. Space and objects around you

Another component of nonverbal communication is the use of space and objects around you, in either office arrangements or room setups. Objects and space affect four sets of choices: seating arrangements, speaker height and distance, use of objects, and dress.

Seating The way you arrange the chairs for a presentation will communicate nonverbally what kind of interaction you want to have with your audience. Choose straight lines of chairs for the least interactive sessions. Choose horseshoe-shaped or curved lines of chairs to encourage more interaction. For smaller groups choose (1) a rectangular table, with a person seated at the head, to emphasize the power of the leader or (2) a round table to encourage equality among participants.

Height and distance The higher you are in relationship to your audience, the more formal the atmosphere you are establishing nonverbally. Therefore, the most formal presentations might be delivered from a stage or a platform. In a semiformal situation, you stand while your audience sits. To make the situation even less formal, place yourself and your audience at the same level: sit together around a table or seat yourself in front of the group. Similarly, the closer you are, the less formal you appear.

Objects The more objects you place between yourself and the audience, the more formal the interaction. To increase formality, use a podium or place a desk or a table between yourself and the audience. To decrease formality, stand or sit without any articles of furniture between you and your audience.

Dress Although the "dress for success" formulas have fallen out of vogue, what you wear does communicate something to your audience. Dress to project the image that you want to create. Dress appropriately for the audience, the occasion, the organization, and the culture. For instance, what is appropriate in the fashion industry may be totally inappropriate in the banking industry. Finally, don't wear clothes that will distract from what you are saying—such as exaggerated, dangling jewelry or loud, flashy ties.

4. Practice and arrangements

The following practice and arrangement techniques will improve your delivery.

Practice techniques Here are some possible practice techniques.

- *Rehearse aloud.* Working from an outline (as discussed on page 90), rehearse aloud and on your feet: "walk it/talk it." Knowing your content and saying it aloud are two completely different activities. So do not practice by sitting at your desk reading your cards. You can't establish rapport and enhance your credibility if you are reading. For an important presentation, practice the entire thing aloud, on your feet. For a less important presentation, practice the opening, closing, and main transitions aloud, on your feet.
- *Memorize three key parts.* A second suggestion is to memorize your opening, closing, and major transitions. These are the times when speakers feel the most nervous and are most apt to lose composure.
- *Practice with your visuals.* A third idea is to practice with your visuals. As we discussed on page 138, become familiar with your equipment; make sure it works and you know how to use it smoothly. Practice to integrate what you are saying with what you are showing and to avoid delivery problems such as talking to the screen.
- *Improve your delivery.* While your are practicing, you can work to improve your delivery by videotaping your rehearsal, practicing in front of a friend or a colleague, or by speaking into a mirror to improve your facial expression or into an audiotape recorder to improve your vocal expression. Use the checklist on page 162.
- *Simulate the situation.* You might try practicing in the actual place where you will be making the presentation or in front of chairs set up as they will be when you speak.
- *Time yourself.* When you practice, you should also time yourself to avoid the common problem of going overtime. Time yourself honestly: say the words as slowly as you would, speak to them in conversation, not as quickly as you would read them; actually take the time to change your slides or flip your charts. If your presentation is too long, edit it. If your real presentation runs overtime, you run the risk of getting cut off in the middle or of irritating your audience.

Arrangement reminders In addition to practicing, another way to gain confidence is to make the necessary arrangements for your presentation so that you won't be flustered upon discovering that you have no markers or too few chairs. All the work you do to create a presentation may be wasted if you haven't made such arrangements. Remember that you are responsible for your own arrangements. Although the janitor, your secretary, or the audiovisual technician can help you out, you are the one who will be suffering in front of the audience if arrangements go awry.

You will deliver your presentation more effectively if you don't arrive at the last moment. Get there about 30 minutes early to check the arrangements, fix anything that may be wrong, get comfortable with the place, and mingle with your audience.

- *Room* First, double-check your room arrangements. Make sure that you have enough chairs but not too many. Get rid of extras in advance; people don't like to move once they're seated. Make sure that the chairs are lined up as you want them and that any other items you ordered are there and functioning. Check the lighting, ventilation, sources of noise, and any other potential distractions. (If, despite your best efforts, a distraction occurs during the presentation, don't get flustered or pretend it's not happening. Deal with it as naturally as you can.)
- *Visual aids* Second, check your visual aid arrangements. Make sure that all the equipment and accessories you ordered have arrived. Test all the equipment far enough in advance so that you can get someone to fix or replace it if necessary. Get the number to call if something should break down during your presentation. Test the readability of your slides or handwriting by viewing them from the farthest chair or asking someone seated in the back row. Make sure that every person in the audience will be able to see your visuals. Finally, check the sequence of your slides and handouts.
- *Yourself* Finally, arrange yourself (as it were). Set up your note cards and anything else you might need, such as a glass of water. Prepare yourself physically and mentally. Remember that you are "on stage" from the moment the first person arrives. The following section provides some specific relaxation techniques.

5. Physical relaxation

When they speak in front of a group, most people feel a surge of adrenalin. In fact, fear of public speaking ranks as Americans' number-one fear—ahead of both death and loneliness. Since most people experience this burst of adrenalin, the trick is to get that energy working for you instead of against you by finding a relaxation technique that works for you. Experiment with the methods explained in the remainder of this chapter until you find the one or two techniques that are most useful for you.

The first set of relaxation techniques is based on the assumption, shared by many performers and athletes, that by relaxing yourself physically, you will calm yourself mentally.

Exercise. One way to relax is to exercise before a presentation. Many people find that the physical exertion of such activities as calisthenics, jogging, or tennis calms them down.

Try progressive relaxation. Developed by psychologist Edmund Jacobson, progressive relaxation involves tensing and relaxing muscle groups. To practice this:

- Set aside about 20 minutes of undisturbed time in a comfortable, darkened place where you can lie down.
- Tense and relax each muscle group in turn. To tense a muscle group, clench vigorously for a full five to seven seconds. To relax a muscle group, release the tension very quickly and enjoy the warmth of relaxation. The muscle groups are: hands, arms, forehead, neck and throat, upper back, lower back, chest, stomach, buttocks, thighs calves, feet.
- Repeat the procedure at least twice, tensing and relaxing each group of muscles in turn.
- Check your body to find if any areas still feel tense; repeat the tense-and-relax cycle in those areas.

Use the Sarnoff squeeze. Speech coach Dorothy Sarnoff advocates this technique.

- Inhale through your nose; exhale through your mouth, making a "sssss" sound and contracting the abdominus rectus muscles, what Sarnoff calls the "vital triangle" just below the rib cage.

Relax specific body parts. For some people, stage fright manifests itself in certain parts of the body—for example, tensed shoulders, a choking sensation in the throat, quivering arms, or fidgety hands. Here are some exercises for relaxing specific body parts:

- *Relax your neck and throat:* Gently roll your neck from side to side, front to back, chin to chest, or all the way around.
- *Relax your shoulders:* Raise one or both shoulders as if you were shrugging. Then roll them back, then down, then forward.
- *Relax your arms:* Shake out your arms, first only at the shoulders, then only at the elbow, finally letting your hands flop at the wrist.
- *Relax your hands:* Clench your fists. Start with an open hand and close each finger one by one, making a fist.

Relax your voice. For other people, nervousness shows itself in the voice. Symptoms include cracking, quivering, and dry mouth. Here are warm-up exercises and some general techniques for keeping your voice in shape.

- *Exercises to warm up your voice:* (1) Humming: Hum slowly and quietly—never forcing the voice—for greater volume. Also, hum with a full range of pitches to open up a greater range for you to use when you start speaking. (2) Breathing: Practice controlled inhalations and exhalations. The exhalation may be a series of short, staccato bursts of air, or one long, continuous stream of air released as slowly as possible. Throughout the exercise, you should focus on the basics of correct breathing, expanding and contracting your diaphragm, not your upper chest.
- *Techniques to keep your voice in shape:* In addition to vocal warm-up, here are some general suggestions for keeping your voice in shape: (1) Wake up two or three hours before your have to speak to provide a natural warm-up period for your voice. (2) Take a hot shower to wake up your voice or to soothe a tired and irritated set of vocal cords. Steam is very soothing and will help your vocal cords shed any mucus or phlegm that has built up on them. (3) Avoid consuming milk or other dairy products before you speak. Dairy products tend to coat the vocal cords, and this may cause problems during your presentation. (4) Drink any warm liquid to soothe a tired voice. Ideal candidates are tea and coffee. (5) Get sufficient rest the night before your presentation; sufficient rest is the best guarantee of a good vocal performance.

6. Mental relaxation

Some speakers prefer mental relaxation techniques to control physical sensation. Here are various mental relaxation techniques to try:

Think positively. Base your thinking on the Dale Carnegie argument: To feel brave, act as if you are brave. To feel confident, act as if you are confident.

Repeat positive words or phrases. Fill your mind with positive words or phrases, such as "poised, perfect, prepared, poised, perfect, prepared."

Think nonjudgmentally. Describe your behavior ("I notice a monotone") rather than judging it ("I have a terrible speaking voice!"). Then, change the behavior by thinking rationally or using a positive self-picture, as described below.

Think rationally. Avoid being trapped in the ABC's or emotional reactions, developed by psychologist Albert Ellis.

1. Here are the ABC's of emotional reactions

   A: Activating Event (such as a nervous speaking gesture) sparks an irrational

   B: Belief System (such as "What a disaster!" or "I must be absolutely perfect in every way; if I'm not perfect, then I'm terrible" or "It's a terrible catastrophe if something goes wrong"), which causes

   C: Consequences (such as anxiety or depression).

2. Transcend these ABC's by

   D: Disputing irrational belief systems with rational thought (such as "Now that I'm aware of that gesture, I can gradually eliminate it" or "I don't demand perfection from other speakers" or "My equipment just broke, but that's not the end of the world. I'll go on naturally instead of getting flustered").

Use a positive self-picture. Many speakers find that positive self-pictures work better than words.

- *Visualize yourself as a successful speaker,* including hearing positive comments or applause. Act out this visualization in your head. Then, act out the role of the person you've been visualizing.
- *Use a positive video picture:* Work with a videotape of yourself giving a real or simulated presentation. Freeze the video at the point where you really like yourself, where you look and sound strong. Then carry that picture around in your head. When it's time for the next presentation, re-create that person.

Connect with the audience. Try to see your audience as real people.

- *Meet them and greet them:* When people are arriving, greet them, get to know some of them. Then, when you're speaking, find those people in the audience and feel as if you're having a one-to-one conversation with them.
- *Remember they are individuals:* Even if you can't greet the people in the audience, think of them as individual people, not as an amorphous audience. As you speak, imagine you are conversing with them.

Transform negative to positive. Consider the adrenaline that may be causing nervous symptoms as a positive energy. All speakers may feel butterflies in their stomachs; effective speakers relax enough to let those butterflies fly in formation.

7. Last-minute relaxation

When it's actually time to deliver the presentation, here are a few relaxation techniques that you can use at the last minute—and even as you speak.

Last-minute physical relaxation Obviously, you cannot start doing push-ups or practice humming as you're sitting or standing there, about ready to begin speaking. Fortunately, however, there are some other techniques that you can use to relax your body at the last minute—techniques no one can see you using.

- *Isometric exercises:* Clench and then quickly relax your muscles. For example, you might press or wiggle your feet against the floor, one hand against your other hand, or your hands against the table or chair; you might clench your fists, thighs, or toes. Then quickly relax the muscles you just clenched.
- *Deep breathing exercises:* This exercise involves inhaling slowly and deeply, then exhaling slowly and completely. Obviously, avoid hyperventilating.

Last-minute mental relaxation Even at the last minute, you may dispel stage fright mentally by using what behavioral psychologists call "internal dialogue," which means, of course, talking to yourself. Here are some examples:

- *Give yourself a pep talk:* "What I am about to say is important" or "I am ready" or "They are just people."
- *Play up your audience's reception:* "They are interested in my topic" or "They are a friendly group of people."
- *Repeat positive phrases:* "I'm glad I'm here; I'm glad you're here" or "I know I know" or "I care about you."

As you speak Finally, here are four techniques that you can use to relax even as you speak:

- *Speak to the interested listeners.* There are always a few kind souls out there who nod, smile, and generally react favorably. Especially at the beginning of your presentation, look at them, not at the people reading, looking out the window, or yawning. Looking at positive listeners will increase your confidence. Soon you will be looking at the people around those good listeners and ultimately at every person in the audience.
- *Talk to someone in the back row.* At the beginning of the presentation, take a deep breath and talk to the person in the back row to force breathing and volume.
- *Remember that you probably look better than you think you do.* Your nervousness is probably not as apparent to your audience as it is to you. Experiments show that even trained speech instructors do not see all the nervous symptoms speakers think they are exhibiting. Managers and students watching videotapes of their performances regularly say, "Hey, I look better than I thought I would!"
- *Concentrate on the here and now.* Focus on your ideas and your audience. Forget about past regrets and future uncertainties. You have already analyzed what to do: now just do it wholeheartedly. Enjoy communicating your information to your audience, and let your enthusiasm show.

II. NONVERBAL "RECEIVING": LISTENING SKILLS

NONVERBAL SKILLS		
Section in this chapter:	**I. Nonverbal "Sending": Delivery Skills**	**II. Nonverbal "Receiving": Listening Skills**
Who speaks most:	You	Your audience
Purposes:	To inform To persuade	To understand
Typical situations:	Tell/sell presentations	Questions and answers Consult/join meetings One-to-one conversations

In the first half of this chapter, we looked at what we might think of as nonverbal "sending" skills—those we use when we are delivering a presentation. In the second half of the chapter, we will consider nonverbal "receiving" skills—those we use when we are listening to other people in a one-to-one setting, in a question-and-answer session, or in a meeting or group collaboration.

Various studies show that businesspeople spend 45 to 63 percent of their time listening, yet as much as 75 percent of what gets said is ignored, misunderstood, or forgotten. Why? In part, because most of us have had little or no training in listening; because we can think at least four times faster than someone can talk; and because sometimes it's hard to avoid jumping to conclusions or becoming defensive before we've heard the other person out.

By learning to listen well, you will not only receive and retain better information, but you will also be more persuasive, because you will satisfy your audience's desire to be heard and you will improve your rapport and your audience's morale.

The following framework for improving listening skills is adapted from listening expert Robert Bolton. The three listening skills clusters include: (1) attending skills, (2) encouraging skills, and (3) following skills.

1. Attending skills

The term "attending skills" means giving physical attention to the speaker, "listening" with your body, either one-on-one or with a group. These techniques will, of course, vary in different cultures. (See pages 29-31.)

Posture of involvement To look involved, your posture should look relaxed, yet alert. Maintain an open position, with your arms uncrossed. Do not stay rigid or unmoving; move in response to what the speaker is saying. When seated, lean forward toward the speaker, facing him or her squarely. One technique to show interest nonverbally is to mirror the same degree of formality in your posture as the other person is using.

Distance Sit or stand at the appropriate distance from the speaker—neither too close nor too far apart. Cross-cultural expert Edward Hall has identified zones of space: in Anglo-American culture, eighteen inches to four feet is "personal space"; zero to eighteen inches is "intimate space." But perhaps the best way to judge distance is by awareness of your audience's comfort level: if the other person is leaning away, you're too close; if leaning toward you, you're too far away. When seated, remember that the head of the table is associated with dominance, and that sitting beside someone may be perceived as cooperative, while sitting across from someone may be perceived as competitive. In one-to-one situations, avoid standing or sitting at a higher level than the speaker.

Eye contact You can also use your eyes to express interest. Focus softly on the speaker, occasionally shifting your eyes. Avoid a blank stare, looking away for long periods of time, and darting your eyes around the room as if you are interested in something else. Avoid such obvious signs of rudeness as reading, looking at your watch, or gazing out the window.

Eliminating barriers To give your undivided attention, try to remove any possible distractions. In your office, for example, you might have your calls held, close your door, and come out from behind your desk. In a group situation, you might come out from behind a podium or table. In addition, watch out for other distractions, such as doodling, tapping your pencil, shuffling paper, or fidgeting with your glasses, rings, visual aids, note cards, and so forth.

2. Encouraging skills

In addition to using nonverbal attending skills, use the following three "encouraging skills" to let the other person speak, and avoid speaking too much yourself.

Door openers "Door openers" are nonjudgmental, reassuring ways of inviting other people to speak if they want to. For example, "All right. Let's hear what the rest of you have to say about this" or "You look upset. Care to talk about it?" In contrast, typical door closers include:

- *Criticizing:* "You get all upset no matter what we do!"
- *Advising:* "I was upset when I first heard of this too, but all you have to keep in mind is..."
- *Overusing logic:* "I don't see what you have to look so upset about. These numbers speak for themselves..."
- *Reassuring:* "Don't worry; I'm sure you'll understand after you hear..."
- *Stage-hogging:* Responding to someone's else's story by telling one of your own.

Open-ended questions One of the main ways to get people to talk is to ask them good questions. The questions designed to elicit the most information from others are known as "open-ended questions"—that is, questions that cannot be easily answered with a "yes" or "no." For example, you are likely to get more extensive responses if you:

Ask	*Instead of*
Tell me about the computer project.	Is the computer project going well?
What concerns you about the deadlines on this schedule?	Can we meet the deadlines on this schedule?
How shall we solve this problem?	Do you like this solution?

Attentive silence and attention Perhaps the hardest listening skill of all is simply to stop talking. Effective listeners must learn to be comfortable with appropriate silence. Silence gives the other person time to think and to set the pace. Hear the speaker out, even if the message is unwelcome. Instead of talking or interrupting, show your interest by nodding your head and using "minimal encouragers," such as "I see," "Yes," or "Uh-huh."

3. Following skills

Once the person has spoken, show that you are following what was said by paraphrasing and sometimes by note-taking.

Paraphrasing content Paraphrasing means restating the other person's ideas accurately and concisely. This will enable you to check the accuracy of what you think you have heard, encourage the other person to elaborate on what he or she has said, and show that you are listening. In a question-and-answer session, it will also ensure that everyone hears what's going on. To paraphrase accurately, you must be patient and hear the person out. Listen for main ideas, patterns, and themes—and then organize those main thoughts as you listen, rather than judging or evaluating first. Next, restate a few key words or summarize the key thoughts or ideas. For example, "So, it sounds as if you are making three suggestions...." then list them or "Seems as though your major concern here is..."

Paraphrasing feelings In addition to hearing what the person says, be sensitive to how she or he says it. Listen "between the lines." Be aware of the speaker's tone of voice, volume, facial expression, and body movement. Empathize; ask yourself what you might be feeling in that situation. Examples of reflected feelings include: "You sound upset about the new policy," or "You seem discouraged about the way your team is getting along," or "Looks like you're pleased with those results."

Note-taking or recording In some situations, you may wish to take notes as you listen. Note-taking can signal that you are really interested and planning to follow up. In one-to-one situations, explain why you are taking notes; generally limit yourself to very few notes, so you don't lose eye contact or your sense of connection; and consider sharing the notes as a summary. In a group situation, you might want to take notes on your visual aids. (See pages 141-143.)

In other situations, however, note-taking may be inappropriate. Gauge the situation to determine whether taking notes will make the speaker feel policed or whether you will concentrate too much on writing. Sometimes showing your concern with full eye contact is more important than recording the facts.

TELL/SELL PRESENTATION CHECKLIST

1. Verbal Structure

1. *Presentation structure (pages 85-89):* Was your presentation structured effectively: opening, preview, clear main points, closing?
2. *Outline (page 90):* Did you prepare an outline, rather than a manuscript?
3. *Questions and answers (pages 91-93):* Did you decide when and how to take questions, and answer difficult questions effectively?

2. Visual Aids

1. *Presentation as a whole (pages 112-117):* Were your visuals well designed for the presentation as a whole: agenda chart, support charts, "stand-alone sense," transitions between charts?
2. *Each individual chart (pages 118-133):* Was each individual chart well designed: graphic charts to show quantitative data, diagrams to show nonquantitative concepts, word charts to show main ideas, typography readable, color effective, avoiding overload and chartjunk?
3. *Equipment (pages 134-137):* Did you choose the appropriate equipment from among multimedia projection systems, still projection systems, animated projection systems, boards and charts, handouts?
4. *Usage (pages 138-143):* Did you use and interact with your visuals effectively?

3. Nonverbal Delivery Skills

1. *Body language (pages 146-147):* Was your body language effective: posture, movement, gestures, facial expression, and eye contact?
2. *Vocal qualities (page 148):* Were your vocal qualities effective: inflection, rate, lack of fillers, and enunciation?
3. *Space and objects (page 149):* Did you use space and objects around you effectively: seating, height and distance, and objects?
4. *Practice technique:* Did you use one or more of the practice techniques listed on page 150 and make the arrangements listed on pages 150-151?
5. *Relaxation technique:* Did you use one or more of the relaxation techniques listed on pages 152-157?

CONSULT/JOIN MEETING CHECKLIST

1. Facilitation Skills: What You Say

1. *In advance (pages 96-97):* Did you prepare in advance by setting the objective, selecting the participants, and setting the agenda?
2. *During the meeting (pages 98-101):* Did you facilitate participation during the meeting by delegating tasks, opening and closing effectively, and encouraging others throughout the meeting?
3. *Decision-making and follow-up (pages 102-103):* Did you make a decision effectively? Did you plan to follow up with a permanent record and an action plan?
4. *Participation techniques:* Did you use an effective technique from pages 104-105, if appropriate: buzz groups, brainstorming, problem-solving method, or nominal group method?

2. Facilitation Skills: What You Record on Visuals

1. *Recording techniques:* Did you use the techniques listed on pages 141-143 to plan, possibly use a scribe, and record comments effectively?
2. *Equipment (pages 134-137):* Did you choose the appropriate equipment?

3. Facilitation Skills: Nonverbal Listening Skills

1. *Attending skills (page 159):* Did you use effective attending skills: posture of involvement, distance, eye contact, elimination of barriers?
2. *Encouraging skills (page 160):* Did you use effective encouraging skills: door openers, open-ended questions, attentive silence and attention?
3. *Following skills (page 161):* Did you use effective following skills: paraphrasing content, paraphrasing feelings, note taking or recording only if appropriate?

APPENDIX A

Formats for Memos, Reports, and Letters

Effective strategy and writing skills (Chapters I through IV) will work in any of the three standard business formats, so memorizing format rules is not essential. In addition, most companies provide their own memo forms and rules for formatting letters and reports. Use the general guidelines in the appendix only if your company does not have its own.

MEMOS

Standard elements of a memo

1. Date
2. "To" heading: reader's name or distribution list
3. "From" heading: your name
4. "Subject" heading: neither too general nor too specific
5. Signature: informal, sign your first name next to the "From" heading; semiformal, sign your initials next to the "From" heading; formal, sign with a closing at the end.

Sample memo formats

To:
From:
Date:
Subject:

Date:
Subject:
To:
From:

Subject:	Date:
To:	From:

REPORTS

Standard elements of a report

Introductory material

- Cover letter or memo. Usually includes reason for writing, authorization for the report, goal, scope and limits, acknowledgments, and audience appeals.
- Title page. Title (summary of focus, not vague generalization), name and position of writer(s) and reader(s), and the date.
- Table of contents. Outlines major sections of the report. Can include preliminary information (numbered with small romans, i, ii, iii), main and secondary sections (pages numbered with arabics, 1, 2, 3), appendixes (usually lettered Appendix A, Appendix B), Exhibits (usually numbered Exhibit I, Exhibit II), and list of illustrations.
- Executive summary or abstract. Summarizes the main ideas. Should make sense on its own, since many readers will only read this part. Should summarize your conclusions, recommendations, or implementation steps, not just say, "Five conclusions are reached."

Body of the report

- Introduction. Builds reader interest, explains why you're writing, previews your organization. (See pages 60-61 for more information on how to write an introduction.) The introduction is not the same as an executive summary or an abstract.
- Conclusions, recommendations, findings, and methodology, organized clearly with effective headings and subheadings. (See pages 52-53 for more on headings.)

Supplementary information (optional)

- Appendixes: supplementary documents such as tables of data, samples of forms, copies of questionnaires, and financial statements. Your reader should not have to read your appendixes to follow your main points in the report.
- Exhibits: supplementary charts and graphs.
- List of illustrations.

LETTERS

Standard elements of a letter

Heading: tells where letter came from and when it was written

- Where: on letterhead paper, at least two lines below letterhead; on plain paper, about an inch from top
- What: on letterhead, date only; on plain paper, three lines: two-line return address, then date

Inside address: tells name and address of person to whom you're writing

- Where: at least two lines below date
- What: *usually five lines:* name, title, company or organization, two-line address; *sometimes four lines:* name and title, company or organization, two-line address

Salutation: addresses reader

- Where: usually two lines below inside address, followed by colon (formal) or comma (informal)
- What: Dear Mr. or Dear Ms. or Dear First Name or Dear Title

Subject line (optional): introduces subject

- Where: usually two lines below salutation, centered
- What: phrase to describe subject of letter

Body: discusses subject

- Where: beginning two lines below salutation
- What: as many paragraphs as needed

Closing

- Where: two lines below final paragraph
- What: closing such as

Formal:	Yours truly,
Semiformal:	Sincerely,
Informal:	Cordially,

Signature

- Where: usually, your signature in ink first, followed by your typed name and title, three to five lines below closing
- What: written signature and typed name and title

Typist's reference

- Where: at least two lines below your typed name and title
- What: can contain your initials in capital letters followed by typist's initials in lowercase; if the letter contains enclosures, enclosure notation goes next; if you are sending copies of the letter to other people, copy notation goes next

  MM:cb

  Enclosure

  cc: Mary Hill

Letter formats

Option 1: Full block format Begin all lines at the left margin.

Company Letterhead

Date

Name
Company
Address
Address

Salutation:

Masthron oltry sirton yotad newbet ekt sretcatahe. Torom hitwed locial koodreoy awit rof resanture of aylow niote criten? Oterbirln omar knille freb doof noidnc. Rewsna 350 gintheoms apn tom forme rekam hos wolloh littlge.

Gnkid tubo ptematt yan norku now lewner oz reay diboter etaryon sellony oiytf nersow. Soger doef retaw ellsw tnemeo stin yo teicor sretem bptse hilpen. Nthron osltry sirton yotad neewbet ehlt sretcat ahc hitwed hip locial koodreoy. Awit rof resanture ao aylow whit nioteco.

Closing,

Signature

Option 2: Modified block format The date, closing, and signature begin to the right of center. Paragraphs start at the left margin.

Company Letterhead

Date

Name
Company
Address
Address

Salutation:

Masthron oltry sirton yotad newbet ekt sretcatahe. Torom hitwed locial koodreoy awit rof resanture of aylow niote criten? Oterbirln omar knille freb doof noidnc. Rewsna 350 gintheoms apn tom forme rekam hos wolloh littlge.

Gnkid tubo ptematt yan norku now lewner oz reay diboter etaryon sellony oiytf nersow. Soger doef retaw ellsw tnemeo stin yo teicor sretem bptse hilpen. Nthron osltry sirton yotad neewbet ehlt sretcat ahc hitwed hip locial koodreoy. Awit rof resanture ao aylow whit nioteco.

Closing,

Signature

Option 3: Semiblock format The date, closing, and signature begin to the right of center. Paragraphs are indented five spaces.

Company Letterhead

Date

Name
Company
Address
Address

Salutation:

Masthron oltry sirton yotad newbet ekt sretcatahe. Torom hitwed locial koodreoy awit rof resanture of aylow niote criten? Oterbirln omar knille freb doof noidnc. Rewsna 350 gintheoms apn tom forme rekam hos wolloh littlge.

Gnkid tubo ptematt yan norku now lewner oz reay diboter etaryon sellony oiytf nersow. Soger doef retaw ellsw tnemeo stin yo teicor sretem bptse hilpen. Nthron osltry sirton yotad neewbet ehlt sretcat ahc hitwed hip locial koodreoy. Awit rof resanture ao aylow whit nioteco.

Closing,

Signature

APPENDIX B

Correct Words

Business writers and speakers should be aware of two conflicting tendencies with language: (1) If you use words incorrectly, you run the risk of offending some readers or listeners. (2) However, language is constantly changing. Words deemed incorrect in one edition of a dictionary may be deemed acceptable in its next edition. Here are some examples of misused and confused words.

Misused words

Word	Does not mean	Does mean
anxious	eager	worried
enthuse	to be enthusiastic	to make enthusiastic
factor	aspect	a cause or contributing agent
fortuitous	lucky, fortunate	occurring by chance (good or bad)
hopefully	I hope	with hope
impact	to affect (verb)	crush together (verb) the effect (noun)
individual	person	single person as opposed to a group

Word	**Does not mean**	**Does mean**
interface	confer, discuss	connect by means of an interface
literally	figuratively, in a manner of speaking	exactly, to the letter
mandate	to command, to order, to require (verb)	to establish a colony (verb) wishes of constituents (noun)
marginal	small	borderline
momentarily	small	borderline
presently	now	quite soon
similar	same, identical	having some resemblance (but possible differences)
via	by means of	by way of
viable	practical, workable, possible	capable of staying alive
while	although, and, but	during the time that

Confused words

accept/ except/	accept: approve or receive except: exclude, make an exception of
adapt/ adopt/	adapt: to change adopt: to take possession
advice/ advise/	advice: counsel (noun, rhymes with *nice*) advise: to counsel (verb, rhymes with *size*)
affect/ effect	affect: to influence (always a verb) effect: result (usually a noun)
allude/ elude	allude: to mention indirectly elude: to escape
among/ between	among: refers to three or more objects or people between: refers to two objects or people
as/ like	as: use before phrases and clauses like: use before nouns and pronouns
assure/ ensure/ insure	assure: to give assurance ensure, insure: to safeguard, make certain
awhile/ a while/	awhile: an adverb (as in *stay awhile*) a while: a noun (as in *for a while*)
comprise/ constitute	comprise: to include constitute: to compose, to be composed of
continual/ continuous	continual: at intervals continuous: without interruption
e.g./ i.e.	e.g.: for example i.e.: that is
eminent/ imminent	eminent: distinguished imminent: about to happen, threatening
et al./ etc.	et al.: and other people etc.: and other things
farther/ further	farther: refers to distance further: refers to time or quantity
lay/ lie	lay: to set down lie: to repose
lend/ loan	lend: to give (verb) loan: the object lent (noun)
oral/ verbal/	oral: by mouth verbal: in words

precede/ proceed	precede: to go ahead of proceed: to go forward with
principal/ principle	principal: main, most important principle: law, truth
stationary/ stationery/	stationary: in a fixed position stationery: writing paper
that/ which	that: use before essential information which: use before nonessential information (usually set off in the sentence by commas)

Confused singulars and plurals

Singular	Plural
agendum	agenda*
alumna (female)	alumnae (female only)
alumnus (male)	alumni (male or mixed)
analysis	analyses
basis	bases
criterion	criteria
datum	data*
diagnosis	diagnoses
medium	media*
parenthesis	parentheses
phenomenon	phenomena
stratum	strata
synopsis	synopses
thesis	theses

*Most people now find it acceptable to use a singular verb with the technically plural forms *agenda, data,* and *media.*

APPENDIX C

Unbiased Language

One of the biggest changes in the business and professional environment has been the increasingly diverse work force. Here are some suggestions for avoiding biased language in your business and professional communication.

Racism

1. Avoid any word, image, or situation that suggest that all or most members of a racial or ethnic group are the same.

   Anglos: prim, cold, stuffy, rational
   Asians: sinister, inscrutable, serene, industrious
   Black: childlike, shuffling, lazy, athletic

2. Avoid qualifiers that reinforce racial stereotypes.

You wouldn't say	**So don't say**
Anthony, a well-groomed white man . . .	George, a well-groomed black man . . .

3. Avoid racial identification except when it is essential to communication.

You wouldn't say	**So don't say**
Pat Buchanan, noted white politician, . . .	Willie Brown, noted black politician, . . .

Sexism

1. Avoid terms that use the word "man" to mean "people."

Avoid	**Prefer**
man-made	artificial
man-hour	working hours
workmen's compensation	worker's compensation

2. Avoid job titles that end with the suffix *-man.*

Avoid	**Prefer**
businessman	executive, manager
foreman	supervisor
salesman	sales representative

3. Beware of third-person pronouns. Here are four solutions:

   - **Reword.**

Typically, a manager at XYZ Corporation will call monthly meetings with his staff.	Typically, a manger at XYZ Corporation will call monthly staff meetings.

   - **Recast as a plural.**

Each employee must decide for himself...	Employees must decide for themselves...

   - **Replace** with ***one, you, he*** or ***she, his*** or ***her.***
   - **Alternate male and female examples.**

4. Avoid sexist salutations, such as "Dear Sir" or "Gentleman." Here are four alternatives.

   - **Use a descriptive term.**

     Dear Customer:

     Dear Subscriber:

   - **Use a job title.**

     Dear Sales Representative:

     Dear Investment Manager:

   - **Use formal non-gender-specific salutations.**

     Dear Sir or Madam:
     Dear Recipient:

   - **Use informal non-gender-specific salutations.**

     Dear Reader:
     Greetings:

Bias against the disabled

1. Avoid mentioning an impairment when it is not pertinent.

Avoid	Prefer
The deaf accountant completed the audit.	The accountant completed the audit.

2. Separate the person from the impairment.

Avoid	Prefer
Bob, an epileptic, has no trouble with the new job.	Bob, who has epilepsy, has no trouble with the new job.

3. Avoid using words that would offend you if you were impaired.

Avoid	Prefer
deaf and dumb	hearing- and speech-impaired
fits, spells	seizures, epilepsy
crippled	disabled
spastic/retarded (unless of course, these words are needed to describe a condition precisely)	

APPENDIX D

Grammar and Usage

This appendix contains an alphabetical listing of common errors and problems in grammar and usage.

Agreement between pronoun and antecedent

1. Make sure that your pronoun agrees with its antecedent. Use a singular pronoun to refer to antecedents such as *person, woman, man, kind, each, either, neither, another, anyone, somebody, one, everybody,* and *no one.*

   Each of the committee members agrees to complete **his** assignment before the next meeting.

   (To avoid possible sexist connotations implicit in the masculine singular pronouns, see page 177.)

2. Use the noun nearer the verb to determine the pronoun for subjects joined by *or* or *nor.*

   Neither Cameron nor Seth has completed **his** (not *their*) memo.

   Either the manager or her subordinates have made **their** (not *her*) group's proposal.

3. Use a singular pronoun for collective nouns.

   The group is preparing **its** (not *their*) statement.

Agreement between subject and verb

1. Make sure that your verb agrees with your subject—which may not be the nearest noun.

   The **risks** of a takeover **seem** great.

   The **risk** of a takeover **seems** great.

2. Use the noun nearer the verb to determine the verb for subjects linked by *or* or *nor, either...or,* and *neither...nor.*

   Either the Art Department or the Editorial Department **has** the copy.
3. Use a singular verb for collective nouns, such as *group, family, committee.*

   The committee is meeting after lunch.
4. Use a singular verb for subjects such as *each, either, another, anyone, someone, something, one, everybody, no one,* and *nothing.*

   Each of us **is...**
   Another one of the members **has**...
   Either of them **decides**...

Comma splices

1. Never put two sentences together separated only by a comma.

   Incorrect comma splice: The company suffers from financial problems, it has great potential in research and development.
2. Watch out for comma splices, especially when you use conjunctive adverbs, such as *consequently, hence, however, nevertheless, therefore,* and *thus.*

   Incorrect comma splice: The company suffers from financial problems, however, it has great potential in research and development.
3. Separate comma splices with a period, a semicolon, or a subordinator.

   Separated with period: The company suffers from financial problems. However, it has great potential in research and development.

   Separated with semicolon, implying that the two clauses are of equal importance: The company suffers from financial problems; however, it has great potential in research and development.

   Subordinated first clause, implying that the first clause is less important: Although it suffers from financial problems, the company has great potential in research and development.

See also "Run-on Sentences."

Dangling modifiers

See "Modifiers."

Fragments

1. Do not carelessly write a sentence fragment as if it were a complete sentence.

   Incorrect fragment, missing a verb: Especially during the October buying season.

   Incorrect fragment, subordinated subject and verb only: When the October buying season arrives.

2. Do use fragments carefully for emphasis, parallelism, and conversational tone.

   Fragments used correctly for emphasis: Out loud. On your feet. With your visual aids.

Modifiers

1. To avoid confusing your reader, place your modifiers as close as possible to the words they modify.
2. Avoid unclear modifiers.

   Unclear: The task force seemed sure **on Thursday** the resolution would pass.

   Clear: **On Thursday,** the task force seemed sure...

   Clear: The task force seemed sure the resolution would pass **on Thursday.**

3. Avoid "dangling modifiers"—modifiers misplaced at the beginning of your sentence. The opening phrase (before the comma) must refer to the subject of your independent clause.

   Wrong: Young and inexperienced, **the task** seemed easy to Lauren. ("The task" is not "young and inexperienced.")

   Right: Young and inexperienced, **Lauren** thought the task seemed easy.

   Wrong: When calling on a client, **negotiation techniques** are important. ("Negotiation techniques" are not "calling on a client.")

   Right: **Salespeople** calling on a client will find **negotiation techniques** important.

Parallelism

Express ideas of equal importance in grammatical structures of equal importance.

- Parallel adjectives

  Wrong: He was sensitive and a big help.

  Right: He was sensitive and helpful.

- Parallel nouns

  Wrong: The new manager is a genius, a leader, and works hard.

  Right: The new manager is a genius, a leader, and a hard worker.

- Parallel verbs

  Wrong: The workers should arrive on time, correct their own mistakes, and fewer sick days will be used.

  Right: The workers should arrive on time, correct their own mistakes, and use less sick leave.

- Parallel bullet points

  Wrong: The president announced plans to

  - trim the overseas staff
  - cut the domestic marketing budget
  - better quality control.

  Right: The president announced plans to

  - trim the overseas staff
  - cut the domestic marketing budget
  - improve quality control.

- Parallel comparisons

  Wrong: First identifying yourself is more effective than to start right off with your sales pitch.

  Right: First identifying yourself is more effective than starting right off with your sales pitch.

- Parallel repeated words

  Wrong: He hands in his payroll sheets, data cards, and his time report on the first of the month.

  Right: He hands in his payroll sheets, his data cards, and his time report on the first of the month *or* He hands in his payroll sheets, data cards, and time report on the first of the month.

Pronoun agreement

See "Agreement between pronoun and antecedent."

Pronoun case

1. Use the proper case form to show the function of pronouns in a sentence.

CASE FORMS

Subjective	I	he/she	you	we	they	who
Objective	me	him/her	you	us	them	whom
Possessive	my (mine)	his/hers	yours	our (ours)	their (theirs)	whose
Reflexive/ intensive	myself	himself/ herself	yourself	ourselves	themselves	

2. Use the subjective case when the pronoun is the subject. Watch out for:
   - Compound subjects

     He and **I** finished the jobs. **We** (not *Us*) managers finished the job.
   - Subject complements

     That may be **she** (not *her*). It was **she who** paid the bill.
3. Use the objective case when the pronoun is the sentence object, indirect object, or object of a preposition. Watch out for:
   - Sentence objects

     The auditors finally left **him** and **me** (not *he and I*).
   - Prepositions

     Just **between you** and **me** (not *you and I*)...
   - Whom: Use for the object of the sentence, subordinate clause, or preposition.

     Whom did you contact at ABC Company?

     The new chairperson, **whom** we met at the cocktail party, starts work today.

     For **whom** is the message intended?
4. Use the possessive to show ownership. Watch out for:
   - Gerunds (*-ing* verbs used as nouns)

     We were surprised at **his** (not *him*) resigning.

- Its and it's

  Its filing system is antiquated. (Its filing system = The filing system of it)

  It's an antiquated filing system. (It's = It is)

5. Use the intensive and reflexive for emphasis. Watch out for:
   - Misuse of *myself:* (Don't use *myself* if you can substitute *I* or *me*.)

     Daniel and **I** (not *myself*) designed the market survey.

     He gave the book to Julia and **me** (not *myself*).

Run-on sentences

1. Never stick two sentences together with a comma, dash, or no punctuation at all.

   Run-on sentence with incorrect comma (comma splice): The company suffers from financial problems, however, it has great potential in research and development.

   Run-on sentence with incorrect dash: The company suffers from financial problems—however, it has great potential in research and development.

   Run-on sentence with no punctuation: The company suffers from financial problems however it has great potential in research and development.

2. Separate run-on sentences with a period, a semicolon, or a subordinator.

   Separated with period: The company suffers from financial problems. However, it has great potential in research and development.

   Separated with semicolon, implying that the two clauses are of equal importance: The company suffers from financial problems; however, it has great potential in research and development.

   Subordinated first clause, implying that first clause is less important: Although it suffers from financial problems, the company has great potential in research and development.

Subject-verb agreement

See "Agreement between subject and verb."

APPENDIX E
Punctuation

This appendix contains an alphabetical guide to punctuation.

Apostrophe

1. Use an apostrophe to form the possessive of a noun or a pronoun.
   - For nouns (singular or plural) not ending in an *s* or *z* sound, add the apostrophe and *s:*

     Smith's account
     women's rights
     one's own
   - For singular nouns ending in an *s* or *z* sound, add the apostrophe and *s:*

     my boss's office
   - For plural nouns ending in an *s* or *z* sound, add only the apostrophe:

     The Smiths' account
     four dollars' worth
   - For hyphenated compounds, use an apostrophe in the last word only:

     my mother-in-law's idea
   - Differentiate between individual and group possession:

     Smith and Green's account (joint ownership)
     Smith's and Green's accounts (individual ownership)
2. Use an apostrophe to mark the omission of letters in contractions.

they are	they're
fiscal 1998	fiscal '98
3. Use an apostrophe and *s* to form the plural of lowercase letters and of abbreviations followed by periods. When needed to prevent confusion, use the apostrophe and *s* to form the plural of capital letters and abbreviations not followed by periods.

b's
M.B.A.'s
J's or *Js*
MBA's or *MBAs*

4. Do not use an apostrophe with the pronouns *his, its ours, yours, theirs,* and *whose* or with nonpossessive plural nouns.

   Their department contributed the financial data; ours (not *our's*) added the artwork.

5. Do not confuse *its* with *it's* or *whose* with *who's.*

   Its filing system is antiquated. (Its filing system = The filing system of it)

   It's an antiquated filing system. (It's = It is)

   She is an accountant **whose** results are reliable. (whose results = the results of whom)

   She is an accountant **who's** reliable. (who's = who is)

Colon

1. Use a colon as an introducer: to show that what follows will illustrate, explain, or clarify. What follows the colon may be a list, a quotation, a clause, or a word.

   The CEO's decision is final: we will maintain an open-door policy with the press.

   The CEO decided we will do the following: generate a list of potential questions, hold practice interview sessions, and give each person individual feedback after the sessions.

2. Use a colon as a separator between a salutation and the rest of the letter, a title and a subtitle, a chapter and verse of the Bible, and the hour and the minute.

   Dear Ms. Wyatt:

   In Search of Excellence: Lessons from America's Best-Run Companies

Comma

1. Use a comma to separate independent clauses joined by a coordinating conjunction *(and, but, or, nor, for).*

    A long independent clause like this one is perfectly fine, but you need a comma before the coordinator and this second independent clause.

2. Use a comma to set off most introductory elements.

    If you find that you have a fairly long introductory element at the beginning of your sentence, use a comma before your independent clause.

    In addition, use a comma after an introductory transition (such as *for example, in the second place, however*).

3. Use a comma to separate items in a parallel series of words, phrases, or subordinate clauses.

    He arranged his pens, pencils, calendar, calculator, and papers on the desk.

4. Use a comma to set off incidental information in the middle of the sentence.

    Incidental information in the middle of the sentence, like this, should be set off with commas.

    Midsentence transitions, moreover, are enclosed in commas.

5. In general, insert a comma whenever you would have a light, natural pause, or whenever necessary to prevent misunderstanding.

Dash

1. Use the dash where you would use a comma when you want a stronger summary or a more emphatic break. Use a dash to emphasize interruptions, informal breaks in thought, or parenthetical remarks—especially if they are strong or contain internal commas.

    Use the dash for a stronger—more empathic—break.

2. Do not use a dash in place of a period or in place of a semicolon between two independent clauses.

    Do not do this—do not join two complete sentences with a dash.

3. Type a dash—with no space before or after the surrounding words—as two hyphens. Most word processing programs have a keystroke option for creating a real dash.

Exclamation point

Use extremely sparingly to express strong emotions.

Italics (or underlining)

1. Use italics for titles of separate publications (books, magazines, newspapers, long musical works) and titles of plays, films, and long poems.
2. Use italics for unusual foreign words; words, letters, or numbers referred to as such; and extremely sparingly for emphasis.

Parentheses

1. Use parentheses for unemphatic parenthetical remarks.

   Unlike dashes—which emphasize the importance of what they surround—parentheses minimize the importance (of what they surround).

2. Use parentheses for defining a new term or new abbreviation.

   The Chicago Board Options Exchange (CBOE) provides more liquidity than traditional over-the-counter options markets.

3. Use parentheses to enclose enumerators within a sentence, such as (1) letters and (2) numbers.
4. Punctuate correctly around parentheses.
   - (If an entire sentence is within the parentheses, like this sentence, place the period inside too.)
   - If just part of the sentence is within the parentheses, as in this sentence, place the period or comma outside the parentheses (like this).

Period

1. Use a period to mark the end of declarative sentences.
2. Use a period to mark most abbreviations.
3. Use three spaced periods, called an ellipsis mark, to indicate the omissions of words in a quoted passage. If the omitted material falls at the end of the sentence, the ellipsis should be preceded by a period.

Question mark

Use only after direct questions, not after indirect questions.

Direct question: What are you doing?

Indirect question: He asked what I was doing.

Quotation marks

1. Use quotation marks to enclose all direct quotations from speech or writing. Long prose quotations—more than ten lines—are usually set off by single spacing and indentation and lack quotation marks unless these appear in the original.
2. Use quotation marks to enclose minor titles (short stories, essays, short poems, songs, television shows, and articles from periodicals) and subdivisions of books.
3. Use quotation marks to enclose words used in a special sense or quoted from another context.
4. Do not use quotation marks for common nicknames, bits of humor, or trite or well-known expressions.
5. Punctuate correctly around quotation marks.
   - Always place the period and comma within the quotation marks.
   - Always place the colon and semicolon outside the quotation marks.
   - Place the dash, the question mark, and the exclamation point within the quotation marks when they apply only to the quoted matter; place them outside when they apply to the whole sentence.

     He called to say, "Your idea stinks!"
     (punctuation refers to quoted matter only)

     I just can't believe that he called back to say, "Actually, I like your idea"!
     (punctuation refers to the whole sentence)
6. Use single quotation marks to enclose a quotation or a minor title within a quotation.

   "Use single quotation marks when you have a minor title within a quotation, such as 'The Star-Spangled Banner,' in this quoted sentence."

Semicolon

1. Use a semicolon to join two closely connected independent clauses of equal importance.

    A semicolon indicates a close connection between two independent clauses of equal importance; these clauses will not be joined in addition by a coordinator *(and, but, or, nor, for).*

2. Use a semicolon to join two independent clauses even if they have a transitional word between them.

    A semicolon indicates a close connection between two independent clauses of equal importance; **however,** don't forget the use of the semicolon to separate independent clauses with a transitional word between them (like *however* in this sentence).

3. Use a semicolon to separate items in a series when your list contains internal commas.

    Use a semicolon to separate items in a series when your list is complex, containing internal commas; when you need stronger punctuation, in order to show where the stronger breaks are; and when you want to avoid confusing your readers, who might get lost with only commas to guide them.

4. Do not use the semicolon to separate items in a list unless the list contains internal commas.

Bibliography

This bibliography is organized by sections of the book. It serves both to acknowledge my sources and to provide you with references for additional reading.

Chapter I: Communication Strategy

Communicator Strategy

Blake, R. and J. Mouton, *The Managerial Grid.* Houston: Gulf Publishing Company, 1994.

Kotter, J., *Power and Influence.* New York: The Free Press, 1985.

French, J. and B. Raven, "The Bases of Social Power," in *Studies in Social Power,* ed., D. Cartwright. Ann Arbor: University of Michigan Press, 1959.

Pfeffer, J., *Managing with Power: Politics and Influence in Organizations.* Boston: Harvard Business School Press, 1992.

Tannenbaum, R. and W. Schmidt, "How to Choose a Leadership Pattern," *Harvard Business Review,* March-April 1958, 95-101.

Audience Strategy

Cohen, A. and D. Bradford, *Influence Without Authority.* New York: Wiley, 1990.

Dawson, R., *Secrets of Power Persuasion.* Upper Saddle River, NJ: Prentice Hall, 1992.

Reardon, K., *Persuasion in Practice.* Thousand Oaks, CA: Sage Publications, Inc., 1991.

Robbins, S., *Organizational Behavior: Concepts and Controversies.* Upper Saddle River, NJ: Prentice Hall, 1995.

Yates, J., "Persuasion: What the Research Tells Us." Cambridge, MA: Sloan School, Massachusetts Institute of Technology, 1992.

Message Strategy

Fielden J., and R. Dulek, "How to Use Bottom-Line Writing in Corporate Communications," *Business Horizons,* July-August 1984, 24-30.

Flower, L., and J. Ackerman, *Problem-Solving Strategies for Writing.* 3rd ed. Orlando: Harcourt Brace & Company, 1994.

Minto, B., *The Pyramid Principle: Logic in Writing, Thinking, and Problem Solving.* London: Minto International, Inc., 1995.

Channel Choice Strategy

Sproull, L. and S. Kiesler, *Connections: New Ways of Working in the Networked Organization.* Cambridge, MA: The MIT Press, 1991.

Culture Strategy

Adler, N., *International Dimensions of Organizational Behavior.* 2nd ed. Boston: PWS-Kent Publishing, 1991.

Copeland, L., *Going International: How to Make Friends and Deal Effectively in the Global Marketplace.* New York: New American Library, 1986.

Culture-grams for the Nineties. Provo, UT: Brigham Young University, published yearly.

Hall, E., *Understanding Cultural Differences.* Yarmouth, ME: Intercultural Press, 1990.

Hofstede, G., *Cultures and Organizations: Software of the Mind.* London: McGraw-Hill, 1991.

Multinational Travel Companion Executive. Stamford, CT: Suburban Publishing, published yearly.

Munter, M., "Cross-Cultural Communcation for Managers." *Business Horizons,* May/June, 1993.

Tannen, D., *Talking From 9 to 5: Women and Men in the Workplace: Language, Sex, and Power.* New York: Avon Books, 1994.

Chapters II, III, and IV: Writing

Ewing, D.W., *Writing for Results in Business, Government, the Sciences and the Professions.* 2nd ed. New York: John Wiley, 1979.

Fielden, J. and R. Dulek, "How to Use Bottom-Line Writing in Corporate Communications," *Business Horizons,* July-August 1984, 24-30.

Flower, L. and J. Ackerman, *Problem-Solving Strategies for Writing.* 3rd ed. Orlando: Harcourt Brace & Company, 1994.

Forman, J. and K. Kelly, *The Random House Guide to Business Writing.* New York: McGraw-Hill, 1990.

Locker, K., *Business and Administrative Communication.* Burr Ridge, IL: Irwin, 1994.

Minto, B., *The Pyramid Principle: Logic in Writing, Thinking, and Problem Solving.* London: Minto International, Inc., 1995.

Murray, D., *Write to Learn.* 4th ed. Fort Worth: Harcourt Brace College, 1993.

Robbins, L., *The Business of Writing and Speaking.* New York: McGraw-Hill, 1995.

Thill, J. and C. Bovee, *Excellence in Business Communication.* New York: McGraw-Hill, 1995.

Williams, J., *Style: Toward Clarity and Grace.* Chicago: University of Chicago Press, 1995.

Chapters V, VI, and VII: Speaking

Anthony, R., *Talking to the Top: Executive's Guide to Career Making Presentations.* Upper Saddle River, NJ: Prentice Hall, 1995.

Bolton, R., *People Skills: How to Assert Yourself, Listen to Others, and Resolve Conflicts.* New York: Simon & Schuster, 1986.

Jay, A., *Effective Presentation.* London: British Institute of Management Foundation, 1993.

Knapp, M. and J. Hall, *Nonverbal Communication in Human Interaction.* Orlando: Harcourt Brace, 1992.

Levasseur, R., *Breakthrough Business Meetings: Shared Leadership in Action.* Holbrook, MA: Bob Adams, Inc., 1994.

Munter, M., "How to Conduct a Successful Media Interview," *California Management Review,* Summer 1983, 143-50.

Sutcliffe, J., *The Complete Book of Relaxation Techniques.* Allentown, PA: People's Medical Society, 1991.

Toogood, G., *The Articulate Executive: Learn to Look, Act, and Sound Like a Leader.* New York: McGraw-Hill, 1996.

Tufte, E., *The Visual Display of Quantitative Information.* Cheshire, CT: Graphics Press, 1983.

White, J., *Color for the Electronic Age.* New York: Watson-Guptil Publications, 1990.

Zelazny, G., *Say It With Charts: The Executive's Guide to Visual Communication.* Homewood, IL: Dow Jones-Irwin, 1996.

Index